This gouache (opaque watercolor) by Italian artist Nicolino Calyo shows Baltimore harbor in 1836 . . . . The view is to the northwest from approximately the site of the present sugar refinery on Locust Point and brings the buildings at right, at the foot of Jones Falls, a bit closer than they were in reality. The steamboat *George Washington* is arriving from Philadelphia at center. On the left is Federal Hill, with its observation tower and signal flags and a glass factory at the base. The 37 by 50½-inch painting hangs at the Baltimore Museum of Art, which first learned of it in 1974 when it was offered from a private collection in Mexico City. The work was purchased by the Women's Committee through funds raised by the Museum's 60th Anniversary Ball.

BALTIMORE MUSEUM OF ART

BALTIMORE HARBOR

A Picture History

BY ROBERT C. KEITH

IN revising this book in 1985, the most startling thing to me was the need to relegate to the past tense—after only three years—such hallowed harbor institutions as Maryland Drydock, Bethlehem Steel's Key Highway repair yard, the Allied Chemical Chrome Works and the Western Electric cable factory. The "deindustrialization" of the harbor, and its ensuing "gentrification," were well underway. Soon after, the very business of the harbor—moving cargo—came under stern challenge, from competing ports to the south. "Baltimore is getting clobbered by the Virginia Port Authority, claimed the *Sun* in 1988. Job loss on the docks moved apace with job loss in the factories, and the proliferation of "service" jobs—seasonal sales clerks and low wage cleanup crews at Harborplace—was no substitute.

How will Baltimore withstand the rapid shift in her economic foundations? Proximity to Washington, D.C., may offer a partial answer. When it comes to filling office spaces, selling waterfront condos and sustaining the tourist flow, she has a place to turn, especially once improved rapid rail transportation binds the two urban centers. Meanwhile ships call, and an invigorated Maryland Port Adminstration is anything but down for the count.

. . .

AS this book goes into its fifth printing, I am honored to welcome the Johns Hopkins University Press as new publisher; my own company is relieved to pass along the burdens of distribution. My first real "publisher" would be pleased also. When Charles M. Connor and I sat down together in the summer of 1982 with rough text and folders of pictures, we persuaded ourselves that the book would command popular interest. Mr. Connor's support was instrumental in bringing the book quickly into publication. Unfortunately he did not

© 1982, 1985, 1988, 1991, Robert C. Keith
All rights reserved
Printed in the United States of America on acid-free paper

First published by Ocean World Publishing Co., 1982
Revised 1985
Johns Hopkins Paperbacks edition, 1991
05 04 03 02 01 00 99 98 97 96   6 5 4 3 2

The Johns Hopkins University Press
2715 North Charles Street
Baltimore, Maryland 21218-4319
The Johns Hopkins Press Ltd., London

Library of Congress Card Number: 90-063441
ISBN 0-8018-4204-2

Illustrations not in the public domain are reprinted by permission of the owners.

Charles M. Connor
1917-1982

live to see his judgement vindicated. He died of heart failure Aug. 22, 1982, before the book was printed.

Mr. Connor was president of John S. Connor, Inc., a firm started by his father in 1917 to provide diversified maritime agency services to freight shippers, steamship companies and others. When he died, his brother, Paul F. Connor, succeeded him as head of the company. One of Paul's first acts

To Mother, and in memory of Dad, who taught us to prowl the waterfront and enjoy the ships.

was to carry through on Charles's commitment to the book. An advisory committee formed by Charles before his death was convened to advise on distribution of the book, and to seek a living memorial from its proceeds. I want to thank the members, who gave of time and expertise: Nancy Brennan, Paul F. Connor, Margaret E. Dougherty, Mary Ellen Hayward, Robert S. Hillman, Sandra S. Hillman, Donald Klein, Daniel J. Loden, George M. Radcliffe, Walter Sondheim, Jr., Jean Van Buskirk, and Henry Weil.

With proceeds from this book and additional monies, the Charles M. Connor Memorial Library Fund was established in 1984 for the annual purchase of maritime books, periodicals and materials for the University of Baltimore's maritime library on North Charles Street.

The logistical help from the Connor Co., and from Paul Connor, Rich Higgins, Bonnie Ciboroski and Jeanette Myers in particular, made distribution of the book a joyful experience.

Subsequent to publication of the book, a number of persons have taken the time to say a kind word, or to share their own personal recollections, or to point out errors or omissions. I thank you all for your comments and help.

The book represents the efforts of many persons, and I repeat my thanks to those mentioned in the first edition; I am glad many could be honored in person at our publication party on Pier 4 in October 1982.

Again I want to credit Laurie Baty, Paula Velthuys and Eric Kvalsvik for their cheerful help in bringing into the book the rich pictorial resources of the Maryland Historical Society, and Lynn Cox and Anne Deckret who provided similar help with the photo collections at the Peale Museum. I also repeat my thanks to Don Meyers, Lucille Langlois, Eileen Kelly, Jerry Smith, of Smith's shipyard on Curtis Creek, Steve and Nancy Smith of the *Gatsby*, Richard Lay and Janet Hardie, then of the Chesapeake Bay Foundation, Fred Kelly and the photo staff of the Baltimore Gas & Electric Co., Dave Harp, Clem Vitek and Fred Rasmussen of the *Sun-papers*, Ben Womer of the Dundalk-Patapsco Neck Historical Society, Don Klein of the Maryland Port Administration, and Laura Brown of the University of Baltimore's Steamship Historical Society Library.

In depth of content, the book owes much to the published works of three pathfinders in the recording of Baltimore harbor history, Robert H. Burgess, H. Graham Wood, and the late Norman G. Rukert, and in appearance to the imaginative map work by Amy Atanat and the untiring production efforts of Judy Jenner.

Robert C. Keith
Baltimore
October, 1990

Powerplant, Pier 4.

EILEEN P. KELLY

Contents

DAVID W. HARP, BALTIMORE SUNPAPERS

Preface

THIS book will take you on an imaginary voyage through the coves and inlets of a wonderful old American seaport.

Baltimore harbor, like the city which has arisen around it, is made of up of a series of "neighborhoods," each with its distinctive maritime history and personality.

We will visit them all, noting some of the major episodes that have marked their past, and the changes that have taken place over the years, some of them rather startling.

For the purposes of this book (and to the anguish of some of my friends), I have given a very broad definition to the term "Baltimore harbor," making it almost synonymous with the entire Patapsco River estuary. Old-timers tend to think of the "real" harbor as the part west of Fort McHenry and Lazaretto Point. But that definition leaves out the busy outer harbor where most of the commercial action takes place today. For historical and practical reasons the book includes the harbor approaches at the Patapsco's mouth, which afford the first degree of protection and the first opportunity for shelter for persons visiting Baltimore by small craft. All of the points listed in the contents page will take on clear identities, from the perspective of the waterfront, as you progress through the book.

The idea for this book arose from my participation on a committee for the programming of the lightship *Chesapeake*. The little red ship was brought to the Inner Harbor by the City of Baltimore in 1981, on indefinite loan from the National Parks Service.

It was evident that the vessel could serve as a base for harbor education programs. But there was a shortage of teaching materials—and especially any materials that would introduce teachers and students to history, economics and all the other factors that make the seaport of Baltimore tick. Compulsion got the better of me in the winter of 1981-82 and I tackled this project. I am by trade an editor and writer, not historian or educator. This is not a textbook, but, to my delight, it has provided a frame of reference for several educational programs.

The first educational user was the Chesapeake Bay Foundation, which moved its harbor evironmental studies program to the lightship, utilizing portions of the crew areas as classroom space to supplement trips on the Foundation's boat *Osprey*. Foundation educators critiqued the book in its development, and later put it to use to broaden the scope of their program.

Since 1983, the book has undergirded an educational program of my own making—tours of the old port section under sail aboard the skipjack *Minnie V*, a classic Chesapeake oyster dredge boat fixed up to carry 24 passengers when the oyster gear is removed for the summer. Under charter to Ocean World Institute, Inc., the city-owned *Minnie V* offers public tours as well as special programs for students, and is attempting to develop a Baltimore harbor field experience in social studies on a par with what the Chesapeake Bay Foundation offers in environmental science. A third educational vessel, the beautiful and impressive *Lady Maryland*, reproduction of the extinct Chespeake Bay pungy schooner, began her program in 1986.

Baltimore harbor offers marvelous opportunities for all kinds of maritime educational activities, and one can only hope that these will flourish as time goes on.

—R. C. K.

Sailing the *Minnie V*.

MARYLAND HISTORICAL SOCIETY

Chapter 1

Queen of the Bay

(Introduction)

Sidewheeler *Columbia* leaving inner harbor nearly a century ago.

BALTIMORE Inner Harbor. What image does that bring to mind?

For the younger generation, it suggests paddle-boats, pleasure cruisers, the smart shops of Harborplace.

But for our fathers and mothers, mention of the Inner Harbor can suggest something quite different. They recall creaky wooden piers, rats scurrying, the deep-throated blasts of steamboat whistles rending the air.

For a century and a half, until well within the memory of many living persons, Baltimore was the steamboat hub of Chesapeake Bay. The shallow waters of the Inner Harbor, traditionally inhospitable to deep-draft ocean ships, were perfectly suited to moorage of the paddlewheel steamers in the heart

of downtown. They poked their noses into the Light Street piers about where the Harborplace food pavilion now sits, or perhaps further south, disgorging vegetables, seafood, and passengers from down the Bay and imparting an aroma and excitement never to be forgotten.

But the history of Baltimore goes back much further than the days of the steamboat. The first Europeans visited the harbor more than 200 years before the steamboat came into being. Baltimore became an important world port in the days when boats were powered exclusively by sail. In this book we will follow the evolution of the harbor from the very beginning to modern times.

It is hard to imagine, looking at Baltimore's jumbled commercial shoreline, that at one time all

Freight bill for carrying 132 barrels of flour from Baltimore to Rio de Janeiro aboard the brig *Ann* in 1838 . . . . The vessel would receive $2 a barrel, half on delivery and the other half on its return to Baltimore.

of it was nothing but trees and fields. Yet that is what Capt. John Smith and his party saw when they sailed up the Patapsco River in 1608. For more than a century after this first European exploration, the river remained a sleepy backwater of the Chesapeake, its few inhabitants concerned with the production of tobacco. The seat of Baltimore County was at Joppa, some 20 miles to the northeast. Even after the founding of Baltimore Town in 1729, followed by Jones Town, Fells Point and Elk Ridge Landing, it was assumed that the main business of the river would continue to be tobacco: growing it and curing it, packing it in wooden "hogsheads" and shipping it to Europe.

Then, in 1750, an Irish-born physician, Dr. John Stevenson, arranged for the shipment from Baltimore of an experimental cargo of flour. The flour was well received in Stevenson's native Ireland. Stevenson arranged for additional shipments, becoming a merchant himself and building a warehouse. He was recognized even in his time as the true founder of Baltimore, the man who saw that it should become the port for America's export of flour. Geography favored this role for Baltimore: she had access to the sea, on the one hand, and to the wheat fields of Pennsylvania and Maryland on the other; and she was very near the "fall line," where rivers like the Patapsco, Gwynns Falls and Jones Falls drop steeply from interior plateau to tidewater, providing a means of power to operate mills.

Growth came swiftly in the ensuing years. A major shipbuilding industry arose at Fells Point and Federal Hill. The first Baltimore steamboat was built in 1813. The nation's first public carrier railroad, the Baltimore and Ohio, was started in 1827, ultimately connecting the Patapsco wharves at Locust Point with the coalfields of Appalachia and the towns and grainfields of the Middle West. Later came the Western Maryland Railroad, connecting with the Norfolk & Western, and the Pennsylvania (now Conrail) which constructed its wharves on the northeast side of the city at Canton.

Well before the advent of the steamboat, Baltimore was the center for commerce on Chesapeake Bay. An observer with a telescope on North Point counted 5,464 arrivals of bay craft in 1796. The coming of steam power meant that vessels out of Baltimore could crisscross the Bay on regular schedules, strengthening the city's domination of the region. Baltimore became "Queen" of the Chesapeake: the principal market for the Bay's produce, the region's financial and cultural leader, the place where Bay residents came to shop.

But Baltimore's influence was not limited to the Bay. Until the Civil War disrupted trade patterns, Baltimore was a commercial gateway to America's South, financing her economy, exporting her cotton and bringing in goods from the North and abroad.

And that was not all. Because of the fortunes of geography, Baltimore became, and still is, the seaport of the Middle West, serving as a funnel through which much of that region's commerce passes on the way to and from the Atlantic Ocean and the world beyond.

Baltimore's fortuitous position astride these three strands of commerce—Chesapeake Bay, the South and the Midwest—made her a natural point for the stockpiling, warehousing and redistribution of goods. It led also to the rise of industries for processing and packaging: canning of vegetables and oysters, refining of petroleum, processing of bird droppings and chemicals into fertilizer, milling of wheat into flour and iron into steel. And so waterfront industry grew hand in hand with waterfront commerce.

In the 1840s, Thomas Kensett, Jr., a young man from New York, set up a small cannery at the foot of Federal Hill. He found a practical method of cooking and preserving oysters and vegetables in tin-coated iron canisters. As a result, Baltimore became the world's greatest food-canning center, a role it held until the present century, when packing houses were established on the Eastern Shore, closer to the sources of supply.

In 1832, Baltimore was the first American city to receive a boatload of bird guano from islands off Peru, on the other side of Cape Horn. One of the customers was Junius Brutus Booth, father of President Lincoln's assassin, who mixed the droppings of the Peruvian cormorants with bone dust which he ground up at his farm in Harford County. By 1865, the Baltimore market was consuming 60,000 tons of Peruvian and Mexican guano a year at the average price of $50 a ton. The noxious material was gathered on the Peruvian islands by convicts and Chinese coolies, each of whom was required to bring five tons a day to a main pile. From there it was put aboard ship by means of a long canvas tube. Crew members wore crude masks of oakum during the loading and could remain in the hold only for 20-minute periods because of the strong ammonium odor. In 1856, the guano imports were supplemented by what looked like guano, but turned out to be phosphate of lime, of volcanic

Tonging for oysters from a Chesapeake Bay log canoe,.... A century ago, when demand for Chesapeake oysters was at its height, some 3,000 small craft like this one were used on Bay tributaries to supplement the harvest of the big sailing dredge boats. Bay oyster production peaked at 14 million bushels in 1887—that's 14 times the present level—and much of the harvest came to Baltimore for processing and redistribution. Canned oysters were shipped to California and Europe. The Pennsylvania Railroad ran them west in special trains, with banners proclaiming "Maryland Oysters" tacked to the cars.

MARYLAND HISTORICAL SOCIETY

origin, from a small island near Jamaica. This material was found to be good fertilizer and provided the beginnings of Baltimore's chemical fertilizer industry. There was always a ready market because tobacco farming so badly depleted the soil. For many years Baltimore led the world in fertilizer production, and several large fertilizer plants can still be found in the harbor today.

Through the years, Baltimore has been an industrial leader in a number of fields. Until fairly recently, the Davison and Mathieson (now Olin) chemical plants on Curtis Bay were the world's largest producers of sulphuric acid, a primary material in the chemical industry. Bethlehem Steel's Sparrows Point plant was the largest steel mill on tidewater. Chrome, sugar and porcelain plants on the harbor were, at least at the time of their construction, the largest facilities of their kind anywhere. The making of those products, along with soap, paint, and a host of other items has provided a livelihood for thousands of Baltimoreans.

Over the last hundred years, the need for space caused the port and its industry to spread downriver, enveloping Dundalk and Sparrows Point on the north side and Fairfield, Curtis Bay and Hawkins Point on the south. The march of industry brought tax revenues and jobs, but has taken a heavy toll on the river. Bottom muds have become so fouled by spillage and deliberate dumping that bacterial mutants are reported by scientists and heavy metals pose a threat to to the food chain. Needed dredging was delayed for a decade because of a dispute over where to dispose of the toxic spoils.

In recent decades, the image of a fouled Patapsco was matched by the image of Baltimore itself undergoing decay and decline, as it faced economic threats common to many northern frostbelt cities. A shortage of strong local philantrophic and industrial institutions seemed to magnify the threat to Baltimore. By increasing degree since World War I, Baltimore has become a "branch-office

MARYLAND HISTORICAL SOCIETY

The downtown waterfront was a favorite gathering place for Baltimoreans long before the advent of Harborplace . . . . The photo at left, taken by David Bachrach in 1867, shows a crowd assembled to watch the departure of a small sailboat on an ill-fated voyage to Europe. Federal Hill is in the background. The photo at right, taken a century later during America's Bicentennial celebrations, shows the visit of the "tall ships."

town." In the World Trade Center building, none of the steamship companies, and few of the shipping agencies, are locally owned. The Port Administration itself is a state agency, although it must respect the city's wishes within city boundaries. Only a few of the major facilities on the shores of the Patapsco are headquartered locally. For the remainder, decisions about the dispensing of civic largesse take place in boardrooms in Chicago, New York, Pittsburg and other distant places. Baltimore Harbor reflects conglomerate America. Even the once powerful Baltimore and Ohio railroad has lost its corporate identity, swallowed up in the giant CSX system and directed from Richmond, Va.

Despite the problems, Baltimore has shown an ability to survive and prosper. Her strength comes in part from industrial diversity. The fact that her economy is not based on any one local product or company has proved to be a blessing in hard times The city also draws strength and vitality from its proud citizenry. It is a city with deep family roots at all levels, from artisan to banker. Its mayor for many years, William Donald Schaefer, became a national symbol of urban regeneration. His elected successor, Kurt L. Schmoke, has focussed on the specifics of providing education and economic opportunity to a populace which is now predominately black.

As ever it has for 300 years, the economic invigoration of Baltimore has its roots on the waterfront. Today, the rat-infested wharves of the steamboat days have been transformed into one of the most attractive public gathering places on the East Coast. The Harborplace pavilions, built in 1980 for less than a third the cost of a single supertanker, generate excitement and hope. "No stranger can go to Baltimore to day without catching something of this resolute city's spirit," Gilbert Grosvenor wrote in *National Geographic* magazine. He thus captured the eternal secret of Baltimore in the issue of February, 1927.

BALTIMORE GAS & ELECTRIC CO.

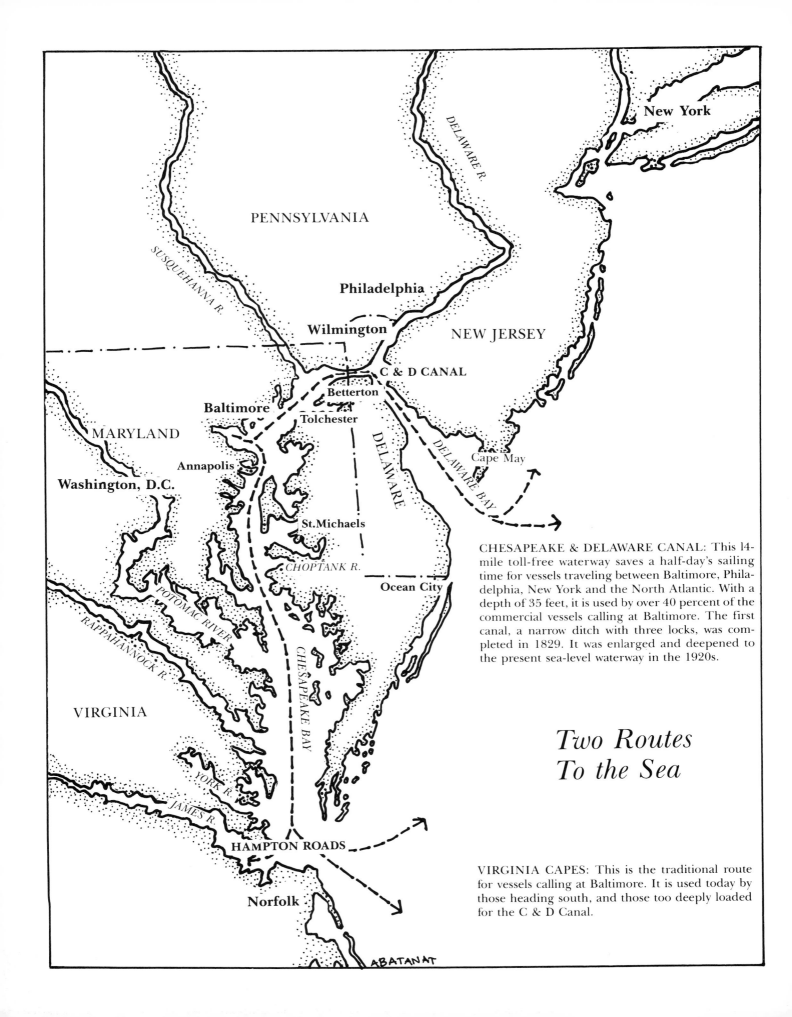

PENNSYLVANIA

New York

DELAWARE R.

SUSQUEHANNA R.

Philadelphia

Wilmington

NEW JERSEY

C & D CANAL

Betterton

Tolchester

Baltimore

DELAWARE

DELAWARE BAY

MARYLAND

Cape May

Annapolis

Washington, D.C.

St.Michaels

CHOPTANK R.

POTOMAC RIVER

RAPPAHANNOCK R.

Ocean City

CHESAPEAKE & DELAWARE CANAL: This 14-mile toll-free waterway saves a half-day's sailing time for vessels traveling between Baltimore, Philadelphia, New York and the North Atlantic. With a depth of 35 feet, it is used by over 40 percent of the commercial vessels calling at Baltimore. The first canal, a narrow ditch with three locks, was completed in 1829. It was enlarged and deepened to the present sea-level waterway in the 1920s.

VIRGINIA

CHESAPEAKE BAY

*Two Routes
To the Sea*

YORK R.

JAMES R.

HAMPTON ROADS

VIRGINIA CAPES: This is the traditional route for vessels calling at Baltimore. It is used today by those heading south, and those too deeply loaded for the C & D Canal.

Norfolk

ABATANAT

A Word About the Port. . . .

THE great competitive advantage of the Port of Baltimore is its geographic proximity to the American Middle West. "We are 140 miles nearer to Chicago than is New York, 289 miles nearer to Cincinnati and 249 nearer to St. Louis," a Baltimore ship agent wrote in 1882, trying to drum up business. A hundred years later, port promoters were using the same pitch. Traditionally, the cost of moving freight overland, to or from a port, was based on mileage, and on that count, Baltimore carries a natural advantage over New York City with respect to many points in the interior.

Despite this advantage, Baltimore saw itself losing general cargo (manufactured goods and the like, as opposed to bulk goods like coal, grain, ore and petroleum) to New York after World War II. There were several reasons: more ships sailed out of New York, reducing delays and consequent pierside storage charges for shippers; the big New York shipping agencies avoided fee-splitting by moving everything through their own jurisdiction; the Baltimore ports, meanwhile, presented a picture of organizational confusion. The biggest problem was at pierside. Baltimore had grown up as a "railroad port" and now, after the war, the railroads were unwilling to make room for the developing truck traffic that was changing the face of American transportation. A ship could dock free at the railroad piers and a railcar was allowed seven days at the Locust Point yards without storage charge. By contrast, when a truck came along with goods for a ship, a charge was levied: $1 a ton to put the goods on the dock, another $1.75 a ton if they had to be moved later. Storage charges were levied after two days. "The worst thing about Baltimore is the piddling charges," a ship agent complained. Moreover, it was difficult physically for trucks to reach the Baltimore piers, and difficult, too, to coordinate pickups and deliveries with the arrival of ships because the railroads would not make berth assignments known until the last minute. On top of all this the railroad piers were reaching a state of decay, and the railroads were neither willing nor able to maintain them.

In 1950 an engineering firm recommended a $129 million program of port improvement, and creation of an eight-county commission to run the port. This report was the forerunner of action by the Maryland General Assembly in 1956 creating the Maryland Port Authority (MPA)* as a state agency. Three years later the new Authority began development of Dundalk Marine Terminal on a former airfield on the north side of the harbor, with the express purpose of accomodating truck-borne cargoes. In 1964, MPA took a 40-year lease on the B & O Locust Point piers (not including the grain pier) and began a $30 million reconstruction program, creating 17 modern berths with accomodation for both rail and truck traffic. In 1967 it purchased, for $1.4 million, the Pennsylvania Railroad Pier 1 terminal on Clinton Street in Canton. MPA set out to make Baltimore a "shippers' port" instead of a "carriers' port." Ships now pay $3,000 to $6,000 a day for a berth, but their shipping customers receive many inducements to bring high volumes of cargo through the port.

Baltimore can never take its competitive edge for granted. The same quirk of geography that puts Baltimore longitudinally west of New York—a northeast-southwest trending Atlantic shoreline—puts the seaport of Charleston, South Carolina, just about as far west of Baltimore. Moreover, Charleston is slung under the Midwest in such a way that it is approximately the same distance from St. Louis as is Baltimore. And New Orleans, on the Gulf Coast, is closer to St. Louis than Baltimore *or* Charleston. A century ago, ship delays caused by long periods of quarantine were a deterent to use of southern ports, but this is no longer a factor. In 1980, the Baltimore port manager for United States Lines complained that it cost $71 to move a cargo container through the Port of Baltimore, compared to $61 for Norfolk and $41 for Charleston. In the 1980s, deregulation of rail rates began to obscure Baltimore's mileage advantage and gave the southern ports new opportunities to lure business through cut-rate deals. Meanwhile to the north, a private company used unregulated shipping rates as a lure for U. S. companies to ship out of Montreal rather than use U. S. ports. And in the West, ports like Long Beach and Oakland, California, clamored to handle cargoes for the Far East. The "rail bridge" from the Midwest to California is costlier than shipment through Baltimore, but faster in reaching the orient by several weeks. So the threat of lost business keeps MPA planners and ratemakers forever on their toes.

*In 1971, the name was changed to Maryland Port Administration.

SOME 31 million tons of cargo moved through the Port of Baltimore in 1989, transported by 2,476 arriving and departing ships, or an average of about seven ships calling every day. The preponderance of this cargo, perhaps 80 percent in tonnage, consisted of bulk commodities: exports of coal and grain, imports of petroleum products, sulphur, sugar, salt, phosphates, gypsum, iron, alumina and other ores. The remainder, about 5.2 million tons, consisted of various items of general cargo, including about 4.3 million tons of cargo packaged in containers, and 404,000 U.S. and foreign-built automobiles.

For the port and the state, general cargo has far greater economic impact—ton for ton—than bulk, because much more is involved in handling it, in terms of longshoremen, truck drivers, freight forwarders, pilots, tugboats, berthing fees, storage costs and the like. It is estimated that revenues from bulk cargo range from a dollar or so a ton for petroleum to $21 for grain, whereas a ton of conventional general cargo means $92 revenue, and the more efficient container traffic brings $72.34 a ton. The average 20-foot container holds about 15 tons and so represents about $1084 in revenues to the port.

In overall tonnage Baltimore ranked seventh in the nation in 1989, and in the handling of containers it was fourth among ports on the East and Gulf Coasts. At last estimate her cargo traffic produced $1.2 billion in annual revenues to the State of Maryland and $500 million in customs collections by the Federal Government.

Observers in Baltimore harbor may be surprised by the relatively small number of vessels of American registry to be seen. The United States emerged from World War II as the world's number one maritime power, but its position has steadily eroded, until today American ships operated by American crews carry less than 30 percent of general cargoes entering or leaving U.S. ports in foreign trade and less than 3 percent of bulk cargoes.

Americans no longer seek seafaring careers, and few have the opportunity to travel by sea. Meanwhile technology has forced the removal of many shipping activities to remote, inaccessible parts of the waterfront. All these factors tend to insulate the maritime world from public consciousness. In Baltimore harbor, you can still go out and see the ships; they are close at hand, and their comings and goings provide a living demonstration that we are still a sea-dependent nation.

The movement of cargo has been accompanied by the construction and repair of great ocean ships . . . . Baltimore has been a leading shipbuilding center throughout American history. (Maryland Historical Society photos)

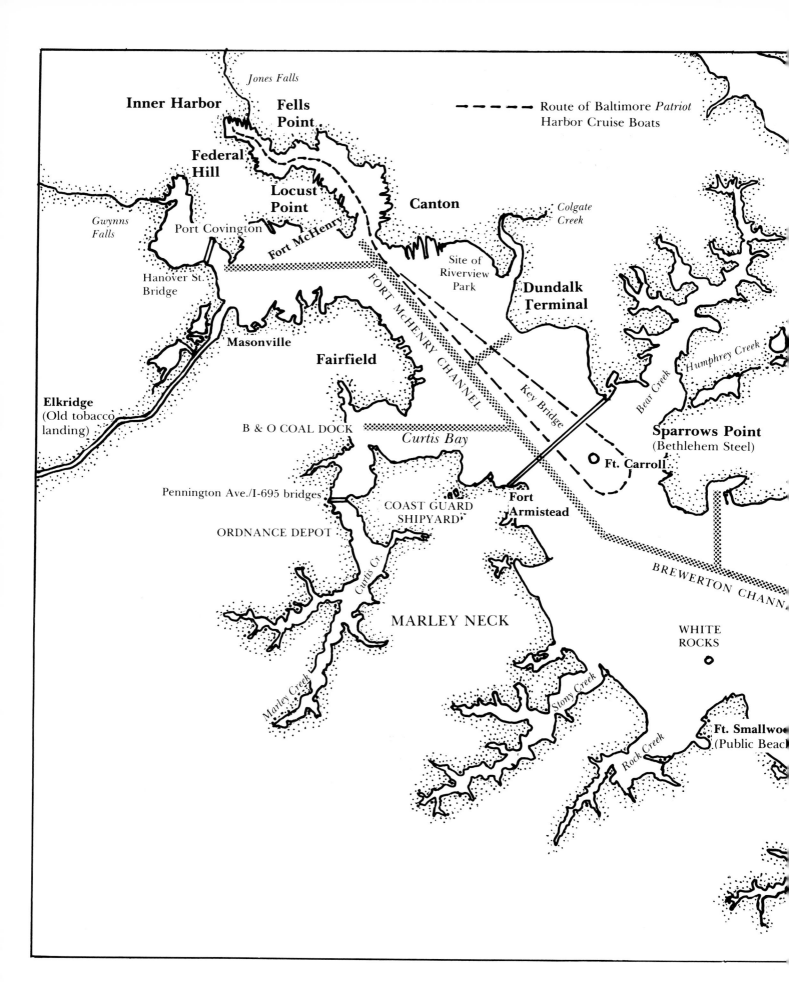

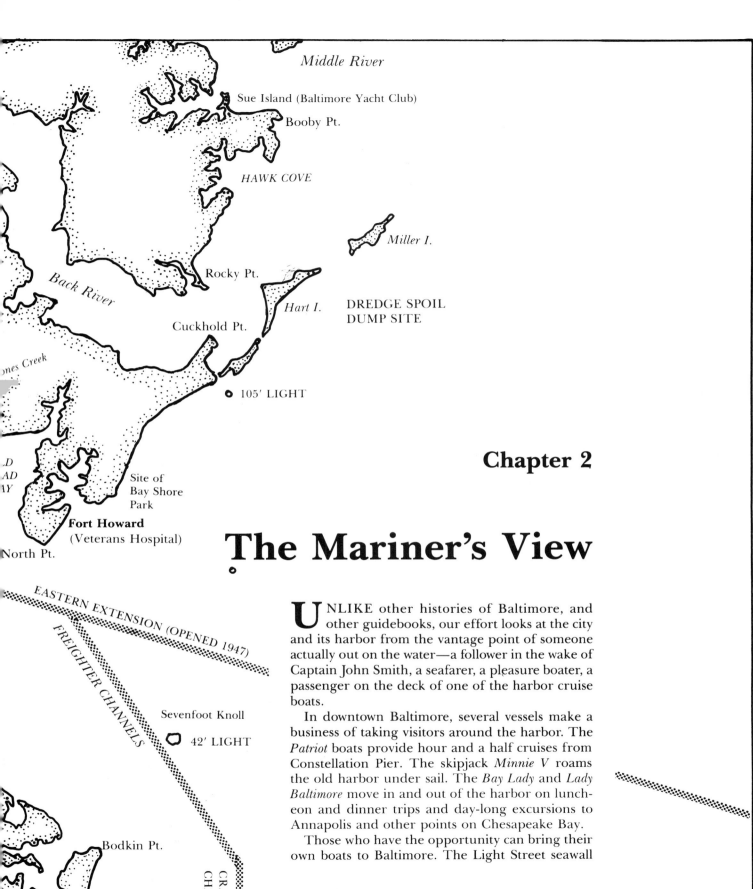

Middle River

Sue Island (Baltimore Yacht Club)

Booby Pt.

HAWK COVE

Miller I.

Rocky Pt.

Back River

Hart I.

DREDGE SPOIL
DUMP SITE

Cuckhold Pt.

nes Creek

○ 105′ LIGHT

.D
AD
Y

Site of
Bay Shore
Park

Fort Howard
(Veterans Hospital)

North Pt.

○

EASTERN EXTENSION (OPENED 1947)

FREIGHTER CHANNELS

Sevenfoot Knoll

⬭ 42′ LIGHT

Bodkin Pt.

CRAIGHILL
CHANNEL

ABATANAT

Chapter 2

The Mariner's View

UNLIKE other histories of Baltimore, and other guidebooks, our effort looks at the city and its harbor from the vantage point of someone actually out on the water—a follower in the wake of Captain John Smith, a seafarer, a pleasure boater, a passenger on the deck of one of the harbor cruise boats.

In downtown Baltimore, several vessels make a business of taking visitors around the harbor. The *Patriot* boats provide hour and a half cruises from Constellation Pier. The skipjack *Minnie V* roams the old harbor under sail. The *Bay Lady* and *Lady Baltimore* move in and out of the harbor on luncheon and dinner trips and day-long excursions to Annapolis and other points on Chesapeake Bay.

Those who have the opportunity can bring their own boats to Baltimore. The Light Street seawall

Paint & Powder acting group on a Patapsco outing.

MARYLAND HISTORICAL SOCIETY

and the old freighter piers in the Inner Harbor have been refurbished and consigned to pleasure boat transient docking. Additional transient space can be found in a host of new marinas pressing into yesterday's shipping lanes along the Canton waterfront a mile or two away.

Until recently, Baltimore was never thought of as a stopping point for boaters. Visions of dirty water, heavy commercial traffic, 14 miles of possible upwind tacking, and limited docking facilities all worked against it. In the 1980s, by contrast, Baltimore became one of the hottest spots on the Eastern Seaboard for yachtsmen to visit.

The emergence of Baltimore as a pleasure boat mecca would come as a surprise to George and Robert Barrie, who introduced Chesapeake Bay to the yachting community in the early 1900s. Their delightful book, *Cruises, Mainly in the Bay of the Chesapeake,* published in 1909, has become a classic. In it, they wax eloquent about the rivers of the Bay:

Chesapeake, from the Algonquin K'tchisipik, meaning "Great Water," is truly a fitting name for the noble Bay whose sparkling waves lap the shores of Maryland and Virginia. This magnificant sheet of water is nearly two hundred miles long, and its greatest width is about one-eighth

of its length, but the Bay itself is not all; numerous rivers, such as the Potomac, Rappahannock, Choptank, Chester, with many others of less imposing size and innumerable creeks . . . total up a greater number of square miles. These latter, really little estuaries, are misnamed, as the word creek is apt to bring to one's mind a dirty little stream running between muddy banks; but this is not the case. They are beautiful, placid indentations with green fields or bits of woodland coming almost to the water's edge and only a narrow strip of beach intervening. Some are very narrow at the mouth, but inside spread out and branch off in different directions. Nearly all of them end abruptly, and one may think he has some distance yet to go before reaching the head, when one is suddenly confronted with a little piece of marsh through which runs a small brook, and that is as far as one can go. The Bay would lose a large part of its fascination if there were no rivers to explore, no bays to sail about in, no snug little creeks or coves in which to drop anchor at night. Providence must have made the Chesapeake early in the morning after a good night's rest and the Delaware late in the evening after a long, hard day, as the latter is all that is mean, unpleasant, low, and aggravating, while the former is the direct antithesis.

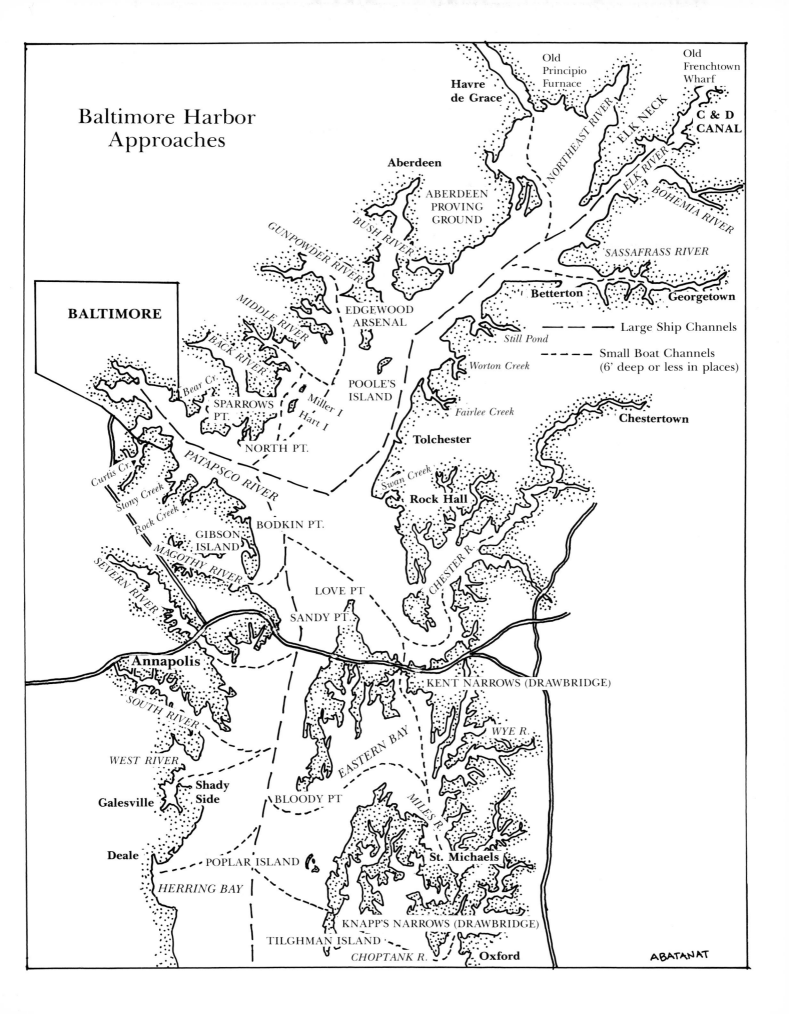

The painful thing about this passage, for Baltimoreans, is that the Barries do not mention the Patapsco River. Nor, evidently, did they ever deign to visit it. Certainly they were aware of the river. In another chapter, they describe a sail across the mouth of the Patapsco while traveling from Poole's Island south to the Magothy:

Here we had a fine piece of sailing; as the wind freshened we ran along with the rail awash and sometimes under. From the Patapsco were coming all sorts of craft—steamers, bugeyes, canoes, skiffs; in short, anything that would float, all laden with mortals bound for Tolchester Beach, to spend the Glorious Fourth and their money.

So the Barries knew of the river and the free-spending, fun-loving people who inhabited it. It could be surmised that the reason they never paid a visit had to do with the way the river lays. It makes no sense to sail up the Patapsco when the wind is blowing from the northwest, or to leave it by sail when the wind is from the southeast. Better to anchor and drink beer. But this is not what deterred the Barries. Visiting Baltimore just never occured to them. With the exception of the passage quoted, where they had been lured off course by shifting winds, they always stayed on the other side of the Bay: "Going down the western shore from Poole's Island to the Patapsco is not safe for a boat drawing more than six feet, as there are unbuoyed lumps. The regular channel is close to the eastern shore."

So there you have it. Coming down from Philadelphia by way of the Chesapeake and Delaware Canal, the Barries clung to the other side of the Bay. Returning from their explorations in the lower parts, they were anxious to get home, and followed the same route. Their book became yachtsmen's gospel, so for decades the idea of visiting the Patapsco was never considered by boating people. Nor was encouragement offered in Fessenden

MARYLAND HISTORICAL SOCIETY

From 1877 until the mid-1930s, Baltimoreans enjoyed their harbor on two-hour steamboat excursions to Tolchester Beach across the Bay. As many as 20,000 a day thronged ashore on the wooden pier, shown at left, from such steamers as the *Emma Giles, Louise, Susquehanna, Annapolis* and *Express.* Patronage fell off during the depression. In 1936, the Tolchester Beach Improvement Co. was auctioned off to bondholders. Its 50 acres, four piers and last two ships, the *Emma Giles* and *Express,* brought $66,000. Excursions to Tolchester were revived after World War II, but the park closed for good after a bankruptcy sale in 1962. At right, ruins of the Whirlpool Dips, photographed in 1966. A marina occupies the site of the old park today.

UNPAPERS: A. AUBREY BODINE

A **R** **Y**

Directions *for* **Sailing** *from* **Love Point** *into* **Potapsco River**

When a little above Love point borrow on the Western Side of the Bay to
[fa]thoms but if you keep in 4 fathoms you will fall upon the Knowls
which lye off Bodkin Point and if you goe into 9 or 10 fathoms you'll be
near the Shoals of Swan Island runn up the Bay in the said depth
untill a Gapp in the Woods on Sparrows point comes within a Small
Sails breadth of North Point (as in the Draught) w.ch will lead you between
the Shoals, in the best of the Channell where is about 3 Fathoms
Water & Soft Ground keep the Marhs on untill the Bodkin Point bears S.S.W.
then Steer W or W by N into the River giving North point a birth of about
a Mile When abreast of North point Steer for the White Rocks untill you
bring Leading point which is pretty nigh Bluff Woods within two
Sails breadth of Hankins's point and so keep it untill you are almost
abreast of the Rocks then Edge to the Southward till you bring y said
Points within a small Sails breadth of Each other which will lead you
up to Hankins's point to which give a birth of a quarter of a Mile there
are several Small Knowls of 3 fathoms on each Side of the Channell which
are Steep too and the Channell between them not above ¼ of a Mile wide

West River

South River

Thomas's

Severn R.

ANNAPOLIS

Tallyp.t

Greenburys P.t

Rattle Snake P.t

Magotty R.

Bodkin P.t

Potapsco R.

Elk Ridge

Belts P.t

The Falls
Ragland

Baltimore
Iron Work
Ferry Branch

Ferry

Curtis's C.r

Ashmans P.t

Limestone

N.W.t Branch

Gossuch P.t

Leading P.t
Swan Gutt
Hankins P.t

Deep C.k

Rock C.k
White Rocks
Rock P.t

Clapham P.t

Bear C.r

Sparrows p.t

North P.t

Back R.

Middle R.

Gunpowder

Kent P.t

KENT

Ferry
Wading Place Ferry

Love P.t

2 foot
2 fath.

Knowls
and Broken
Ground

Swan Is.t

Snaw P.t

Bodkin P.t
Parsens P.t

Wye River

Marsh
Long Neck
Thoroughfare

Grays Inn C.k

Langfords Bay

Courseys

Queens Town

Reeds C.k

Corsica C.k

Comegys P.t

Old Town
Ferry

Baals C.r

Millett

Ogle Town

S.o E. Branch

Chester R.

Farlo C.r

Worton C.r

Churn C.r
Steel Pone C.r

Chester Town

Sassafras R.

Bools P.t

Buf

N **D**

There's no better way to see the Patapsco than by sailing ship . . . . A crew of two or three would suffice for a schooner of this size in commerce. The large crew here marks this as some kind of pleasure or training voyage, or perhaps a race. How many people do you count?

MARYLAND HISTORICAL SOCIETY

Blanchard's *A Cruising Guide to the Chesapeake* which through many editions described the upper Patapsco as "too commercial" and wrote off the Northwest Branch, or inner harbor, as being "of little interest to yachtsmen."

Even today, the Patapsco seems out of the way for boaters coming from the north, down the eastern shore channel. To visit Baltimore seems like doubling back. But for those coming up from the south, the prospect is different. Once you pass under the Chesapeake Bay Bridge at Sandy Point, it is just as convenient to continue straight ahead, to the Patapsco, as it is to veer off to the right, toward Rock Hall, Tolchester and the head of the Bay. Another appealing approach to the Patapsco is from the southeast, out of Eastern Bay, through Kent Narrows, past Love Point and across the main Bay to the river. The Love Point approach is detailed in the map at left, drawn during the colonial era.

Either way, coming up from the south, or across the Bay from Love Point, the boater must head for Bodkin Point, the first landmark at the entrance to the river. Once Bodkin Point is cleared, the boater is home free to downtown Baltimore, about 14 miles due northwest. Whether the voyage is a true one, from the deck of a boat with sun and spray in the face, or an imaginery one, in the security of a properly oriented armchair, the voyager will be curious about what lies up the smaller bays and creeks that lead off the main river and what transpires at the awesome commercial installations. Many of the answers will be found on the following pages.

This 1735 map gives sailing instructions for approaching the Patapsco River from the Chester River and Love Point across the Bay . . . . The river is shown wide and deep up to Elk Ridge Landing, which was the chief tobacco port in those days. The mapmaker, sea captain Walter Hoxton, did not bother to draw in the "Northwest Branch" where downtown Baltimore and the Inner Harbor are located today. (Maryland Historical Society)

Bodkin Creek, looking south. Bodkin Point is at left, out of picture.

Chapter 3

The Pleasure Creeks

GREENHORNE & O'MARA, INC.

THREE creeks at the lower mouth of the Patapsco—Bodkin, Rock and Stony—have so far been spared the rude intrusion of industry. Residents enjoy a lifestyle of fishing, crabbing and pleasure boating. The names of the communities— Bayside Beach, Alpine Beach, Paradise Beach, Venice on the Bay, Fairhaven Beach, Orchard Beach—recall past days of glory when they were the summer swimming holes of Baltimore. That

was before the Bay Bridge was built and the Atlantic Ocean was brought within a four-hour drive.

In this aerial view, wooded Bodkin Creek spreads its tentacles in five directions inland from its narrow mouth, offering snug anchorage at every hand. The creek has sheltered many a working oyster fleet in years past. Today the shore is lined with small docks and private residences, whose occupants delight in their ready access to the open

Bay, even if it does mean an hour's drive to work every day. For visitors, the creek offers gas and a few supplies, but no restaurants or other attractions save safe anchorage.

Ventnor's Marina at Graveyard Point stands on a site used by the City of Baltimore in the 1920s to set up a large piggery for garbage disposal. The idea was to barge the city's garbage to Bodkin Creek and feed it to 15,000 pigs. The city bought 160 acres, built a wharf, laid concrete floors for the piggery and began the barging, but when the first pigs went to slaughter the contractor abandoned the project and disappeared with $15,000.

Another contractor built a reduction plant just across at Spit Point where he cooked garbage into grease and sold it to the soap companies. The operation was discontinued in the 1930s under pressure from residents disgusted with the odors.

Bodkin Creek is a base for the Maryland Marine Police, known in its early days as the "Oyster Navy" because of its fights to keep "pirates" off the Bay oyster beds. Officer K. L. Phillips won immortality at his Bodkin post in 1966 when he filed this brief report: "Found bottom half of girl's bathing suit at Bodkins Point. Returned same to owner. Had no trouble locating her. Very little activity this date."

PHOTO BY AUTHOR

Hancock House

Hancock House, at Bayside Beach on the west side of the Bodkin Creek entrance, is said to be the oldest structure in Maryland north of the Severn River.

The stone house was built by Stephen Hancock, a British military officer, who was sent up from St. Mary's City in the mid-1600s to guard the Patapsco as a result of warfare between the Seneca and Susquehanna Indians. Hancock was assisted in the construction of the house by Susquehannas who came in for protection.

The house remained the home of a Hancock for three hundred years, until 1962, when it was willed to the Historic Annapolis society. It was opened to

the public for a time, then closed and boarded up for want of funds, which is its unfortunate status today.

Hancock House played an important role in the the War of 1812, when it was the home and headquarters of Captain Francis Hancock. Whenever the British fleet came above Annapolis, Hancock would raise a signal flag, which signal was in turn taken up at Steeple House Farm above North Point, on the other side of the Patapsco, where it could be seen from the observatory at Federal Hill in downtown Baltimore. The timely warnings had much to do with the successful defense of the city at Fort McHenry in 1814.

Disappearing Lighthouse

Now you see it, now you don't . . . . On navigation charts, the approach to Bodkin Point from Chesapeake Bay shows every element of a Coast Guard safe boating quiz: one "rky," two "obstr," two wreck symbols, one "hrd," one place showing only a foot of water, two splotches of land awash and another place with "yl S" which evidently signifies yellow sand for anyone unfortunate enough to sample it. In the midst of all this, the chart shows submerged "Ruins," spelled out with the vowels, perhaps for extra drama.

The explanation is that Bodkin Point once extended further into the Bay and held at its tip the large rock light and tender's house shown in the 1913 photo at right. Within only the last 40 years or so, the entire complex has collapsed and washed away or slipped beneath the surface. The total submergence of the building stones, along with six-foot granite slabs used in a seawall, gives weight to claims of scientists that the waters of the Chesapeake Bay are rising 1 to 1¾ inches every ten years. The changes over an 80-year period can be seen by comparing the two charts below.

The sunken rocks pose a continuing hazard; every year, boats of unwary travelers are towed into Bodkin Creek marinas for repairs. The hidden dangers can be avoided by steering to the east of a pole with a green marker and green flashing light, but the Bodkin Creek entrance is marked by three poles with green markers, two of which have green

MARYLAND HISTORICAL SOCIETY

Bodkin Light, 1913.

flashing lights, and yl S to the boater who guides by the wrong marker. Boaters can resolve all doubts by steering a few hundred yards further east into the steamer channel, but that invites a different kind of adventure. Residents would like to see the rocks scooped into a pile and marked, or removed altogether.

NATIONAL OCEAN SURVEY

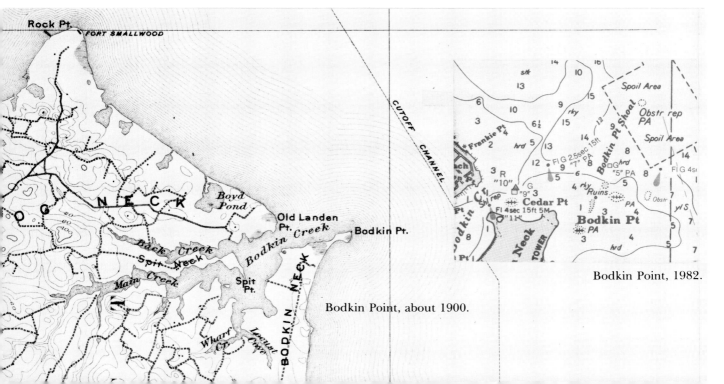

Bodkin Point, about 1900.

Bodkin Point, 1982.

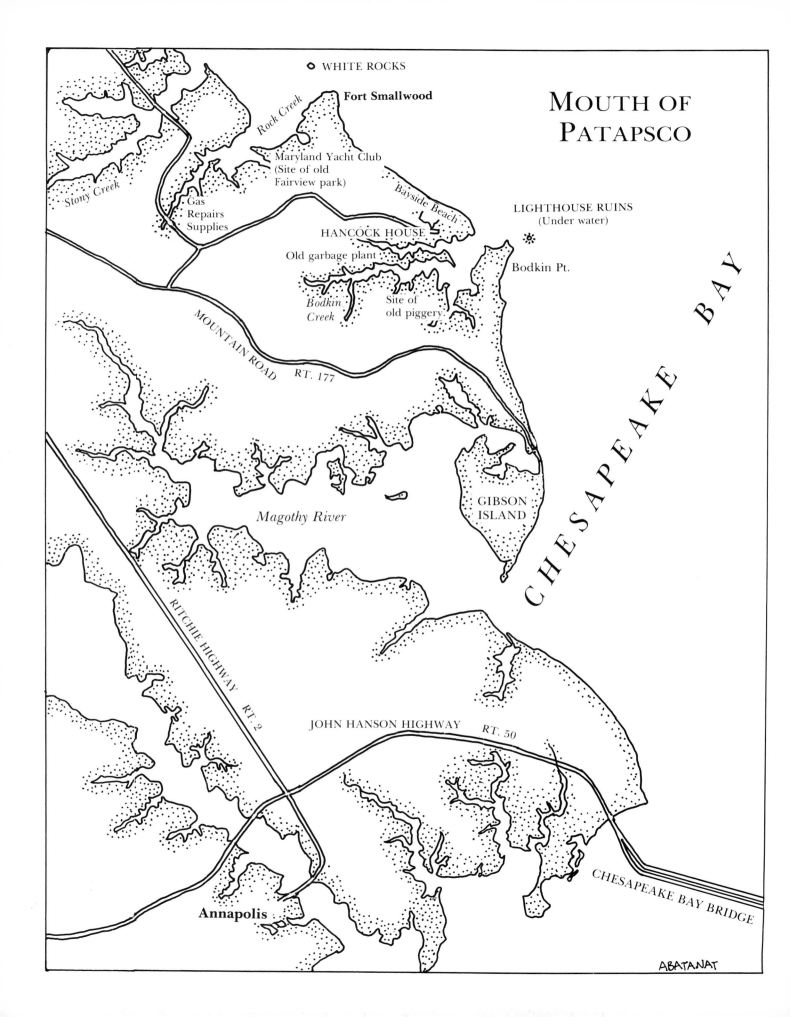

White Rocks ⬦

WHITE ROCKS

Fort Smallwood

Rock Creek

Maryland Yacht Club
(Site of old
Fairview park)

Stony Creek

Gas
Repairs
Supplies

Bayside Beach

LIGHTHOUSE RUINS
(Under water)

HANCOCK HOUSE

Old garbage plant

Bodkin Pt.

Bodkin
Creek

Site of
old piggery

MOUTH OF PATAPSCO

MOUNTAIN ROAD

RT. 177

CHESAPEAKE BAY

GIBSON
ISLAND

Magothy River

RITCHIE HIGHWAY   RT. 2

JOHN HANSON HIGHWAY   RT. 50

Annapolis

CHESAPEAKE BAY BRIDGE

ABATANAT

White Rocks, off Rock Creek.

PHOTO BY AUTHOR

Rock, Stony Creeks

THE Indian name "Patapsco" first appears on land grants of about 1655. According to one source, it is derived from "Pota"—to jut out, to bulge; "psk"—a ledge of rock; and the locative "ut"—at; hence "Pota-psk-ut"—at the jutting ledge of rock . . . probably referring to the "White Rocks," a startling outcropping of sandstone rocks in the river near the point where Rock Creek enters.

Rock Creek derives its name from these rocks, just as Stony Creek, a short distance to the west, is named for a heap of brown rocks at its mouth, believed to be of the same geologic strata. These two creeks are the last non-industrial waters on the way into Baltimore harbor. Heavily populated, they are dotted with small-boat marinas and private docks. Rock Creek is favored for overnight anchorage. Fort Smallwood, at Rock Point on the creek's mouth, is a 100-acre public park operated by the City of Baltimore, which purchased it from the Federal Government for $55,000 in 1926. It was established as a fort in 1896, but few traces remain.

From around 1900 until the second world war, the Rock Creek Steamship Co. ran steamers to beaches and amusement parks on the two creeks from Baltimore's inner harbor. A principal stop was Fairview, a small amusement park just inside the mouth of Rock Creek which, like the park at Tolchester across the Bay, was much favored by Sunday School groups because no alcohol was sold on the grounds. The Maryland Yacht Club took over Fairview Park in 1945.

On Sept. 7, 1978, a wrecking crane dismantled the 136-foot paddlewheel steamer *Kitty Knight*, ex. *Van Corlaer the Trumpeter*, from a muddy bed in Rock Creek where she had lain abandoned for 54 years. Another Rock Creek steamer, the *Avalon*, renamed the *Federal Hill* in 1937, was cut down to a barge in 1940 and continued to visit Baltimore for a number of years. (Photo page 89)

Rock Creek from Maryland Yacht Club.

PHOTO BY AUTHOR

Downtown skyline Dundalk Marine Terminal
Hawkins Point Marine Terminal Francis Scott Key Bridge

Chapter 4

Hawkins Point

AS YOU move upriver from Stony Creek you pass Marley Neck, the most grim and desolate section of the Patapsco shoreline. If the future brings more expansion of waterfront industry, the sites will surely be found here. Tall smokestacks already mark the shoreline. Immediately west of Stony Creek is the Herbert A. Wagner plant of the Baltimore Gas & Electric Co., followed by the company's new Brandon Shores plant with its blinking strobelights. Then after about a mile and a half of featureless waterfront comes the giant Cox Creek copper refinery, then the Glidden paint factory bathed in the white dust of titanium dioxide. By this time you are at Hawkins Point which, in keeping with the gloomy atmosphere here, has become

the toxic waste dump for Baltimore harbor industry. The Francis Scott Key Bridge, carrying Beltway (I-695) traffic over the Patapsco River, was opened here in 1978. Immediately west of the bridge is the Maryland Port Administration's Hawkins Point Terminal. The pier was erected during World War II as a terminal for loading ammunition. It was virtually destroyed by fire in 1951. In 1958 the Port Administration purchased the damaged pier and 137 acres of adjoining land for $1,510,000, rebuilt the pier and leased it to the B & O Railroad to bring Chilean blister copper to the nearby refinery (then owned by Kennecott). Later the pier was revamped to receive and store alumina for the Eastalco Aluminum Co. of Frederick, Maryland.

EILEEN P. KELLY

This splendid panoramic view from Fort Armistead on Hawkins Point attracts a steady procession of visitors. In 1983-84 the City of Baltimore spruced up the 45-acre park, installing a two-lane boat launching ramp, a fishing pier, paved walks and picnic tables. The park is reached from Fort Smallwood road.

Other industries in the neighborhood include the plant and receiving pier of the U.S. Gypsum Corp., upriver on Leading Point, and the Davison Chemical plant further up on Sledds Point. Immediately inland from these plants is the waste dump, operated by the State of Maryland, which was once a repository for chemical residues from Glidden, Browning Ferris Industries, QC Corp. and others. In 1982 a portion of the dump was closed and materials were dug up and removed. But the tract continued to receive chrome wastes from the Allied plant in the Inner Harbor.

In 1985 the City of Baltimore opened a 156-acre landfill west of the State landfill, so as to receive bulk trash as well as ash from a downtown incineration plant. As a Baltimore *Evening Sun* writer commented in 1975, "It is not an area in which anything much worse can happen than has already occurred. . ."

Twenty-two homeowners in the tiny community of Hawkins Point, just across the highway south of the landfills, felt increasing anguish as the dumping spread. In 1982 Gov. Harry Hughes agreed to spend $1.5 million to buy them out, rather than incur the millions more it would cost to provide pure water, sewage and other amenities in the face of the industrial encroachment.

We touch briefly on several aspects of Hawkins Point history, none of them cheerful, and quickly move on.

SUNPAPERS

On Jan. 10, 1951, a ten-alarm fire engulfed the old Hawkins Point ammunition pier while it was being used as a staging area for construction of the Chesapeake Bay Bridge at Sandy Point . . . . The $15 million loss made the fire the worst in the harbor since the great Baltimore fire of 1904. Included in the loss was the 25,000-ton decommissioned troop transport *George Washington* which was tied up at the pier when the fire broke out. The German-built *George Washington* was the "peace ship" that carried President Wilson to the Versailles peace conference after World War I. It carried 250,000 U.S. troops in World War II. Fire damage was so extensive that the ship was towed over to the Boston Metals Co. in Curtis Bay and scrapped.

Alum Chine

AT 10:30 a..m. on March 7, 1913, the Welsh freighter *Alum Chine* blew up off Hawkins Point while loading 500 tons of dynamite for use in construction of the Panama Canal. It was the worst shipping disaster in the history of Baltimore harbor. Thirty-three men were killed and 60 injured. The 1,800-ton freighter and two railroad "carfloat" barges tied up alongside were torn to pieces and sent to the bottom of the harbor, along with six railroad boxcars which carried the boxes of dynamite aboard the barges. The tugboat *Atlantic* was damaged and sank while trying to escape. The explosion broke windows throughout Baltimore and as far away as Havre de Grace and Chestertown. Earth tremors were felt in Philadelphia, Dover, Del., and Atlantic City.

According to accounts, stevedores and crew members were transferring the wooden cases of dynamite from the railroad boxcars to the ship by hand when a foreman rammed his hook into a case of dynamite that had been placed crookedly. The dynamite caught fire, at first giving off dense smoke. Seven minutes later the explosion came.

The freighter's steward, John W. Forrest, jumped overboard at the first sign of fire and was picked up by a nearby motor launch. "As the launch then raced on away from the *Alum Chine*, which by now was belching huge clouds of smoke, there suddenly was a deafening report," he later wrote. "It seemed to go dark as night and debris began falling all around us. When that rain stopped there was simply nothing at all where our ship had been, but from her position a white-crested wave as big as a mountain was coming at us, and when it struck it

PEALE MUSEUM

lifted our little boat in the air and tumbled us all over each other, leaving us bruised, wet, and numb with cold....Soon, hundreds of seagulls came to feast on the thousands of fish the blast had killed." By chance, photographer Alfred Waldeck happened to be out in the harbor at the time of the explosion, and caught the remarkable mushroom cloud picture above.

In 1976, workers of the A. Smith & Sons shipyard on Curtis Creek were laying a water main in the harbor when they brought up this severely bent connecting rod and other wreckage believed to be from the *Alum Chine.*

PHOTO BY AUTHOR

27

PHOTOS BY AUTHOR

The River Forts

Fort Armistead, along with Forts Howard (at North Point) and Smallwood (at Rock Point) was built at the time of the Spanish-American War, when there was genuine concern that foreign battleships could sail up Chesapeake Bay and penetrate the harbor . . . . Crushed granite used in the cement makes the gun emplacements almost indestructable. The cannons were removed to Fort Howard around 1903 after the nearby Davison Chemical Co. complained that practice firing was causing leaks in sulphuric acid tanks. The Army abandoned the fort altogether in 1921 and turned it over to the City of Baltimore for use as a park. The Federal Government has reclaimed it twice since then, during World War II as part of its Hawkins Point ammunition dump, and in the 1950s as the site of an anti-aircraft battery. Today the sunken fortifications are again overgrown with weeds and vines.

Fort Carroll in 1911, armed with cannon.

MARYLAND HISTORICAL SOCIETY

MARYLAND HISTORICAL SOCIETY

Fort Carroll, an artificial island in the harbor across from Fort Armistead, was constructed about 1850 under the direction of Robert E. Lee, then a Colonel in the Federal Army . . . . The four-acre stone fortress was intended to have four tiers of cannon ports but work was halted when it was two tiers high, and then the second tier was cut back during a "modernization" program in the 1890s, before these photos were taken. The fort never served any real military purpose (weapons advances made it vulnerable even before construction could be finished) and no one seems to know what to do with it today. A Baltimore attorney, Benjamin N. Eisenberg, purchased it from the Army in 1958 for $10,000, had it fixed up and opened it to the public for several years. But plans for a restaurant failed to materialize and the fort was closed. Signs warn visitors away. They should be heeded. The rock landing place can cause damage to boats. Inside the fort, unlit gun emplacements harbor dangerous pits and dropoffs.

Schooner passing Fort Carroll in late 1890s, aided by its yawl boat.

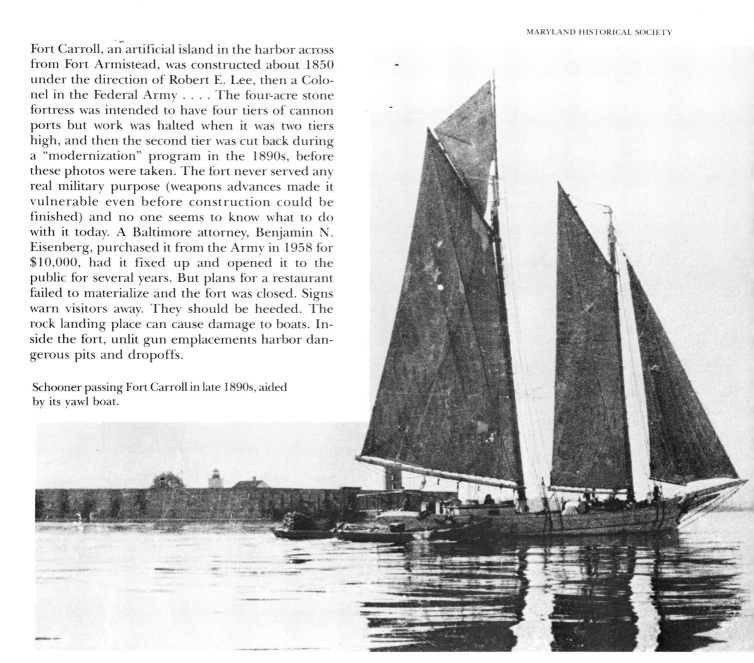

BALTIMORE GAS & ELECTRIC COMPANY PHOTO

The Davison Chemical Co. has operated in the Hawkins Point area since 1900. . . . . The company was founded in 1826 when William Davison opened a plant at what is now the bottom of Druid Lake. The company subsequently established plants at Canton and Hawkins Point and began development of the present 271-acre site in 1909. It became a division of W. R. Grace & Co. in 1954. For many years this plant was the world's leading producer of sulphuric acid and of phosphate rock fertilizer (superphosphate). Both activities were eventually phased out as the company undertook the production of more sophisticated chemicals. Contemporary products include silica gel, used in food, cosmetics, paint (as a flatting agent) and in packaging of instruments (to absorb moisture); "molecular sieves" used to purify natural gas; cracking caltalyst additives used in refining petroleum; and catalysts for auto emission control devices. The "auto cat" plant, identifiable by the four silos and "Grace" sign, is the world's largest. Protruding from the water at the upper right of photo are hulks of 15 World War I wooden freighters and the smokestack of the *District of Columbia,* discussed in the next chapter.

Quarantine Station

THIS collection of stately buildings included a detention barracks, a "leper house" and a "delousing plant"—all part of the Quarantine Station that stood on Leading Point, just west of Hawkins Point, from about 1870 to 1961. The station was successor to the Lazaretto Point "pesthouse" (page 138) and was intended to protect the nation against contagious diseases brought in from overseas.

The Quarantine Station was operated by the City of Baltimore until the federal Public Health Service took it over in 1918. Worldwide reduction of diseases led to a phasing out of the operation, with the last ship inspections taking place around 1975. The quarantine office was transferred to the downtown Custom House in 1961, and then to Baltimore-Washington Airport and later to Dulles Airport west of Washington, D.C. A quarantine service operated by the federal Agricultural Dept. continues to board arriving ships at dockside to check for animal and plant diseases.

In 1963, the Maryland Port Administation purchased the old Quarantine Station tract, including a number of unmarked graves, for $269,500. Nothing remains of the buildings today.

Ships arriving from foreign ports were required to stand off the Quarantine Station while health officials came aboard and checked out passengers and crew . . . . The photo below shows officials from the quarantine boat *T. B. Mc-Clintic* boarding what appears to be an oil barge in 1949. The Customs Service also boarded most ships before they reached dock in those days. At right, a customs officer goes up a "Jacobs ladder" dangling over the side of a freighter in 1948. Maryland Historical Society photos.

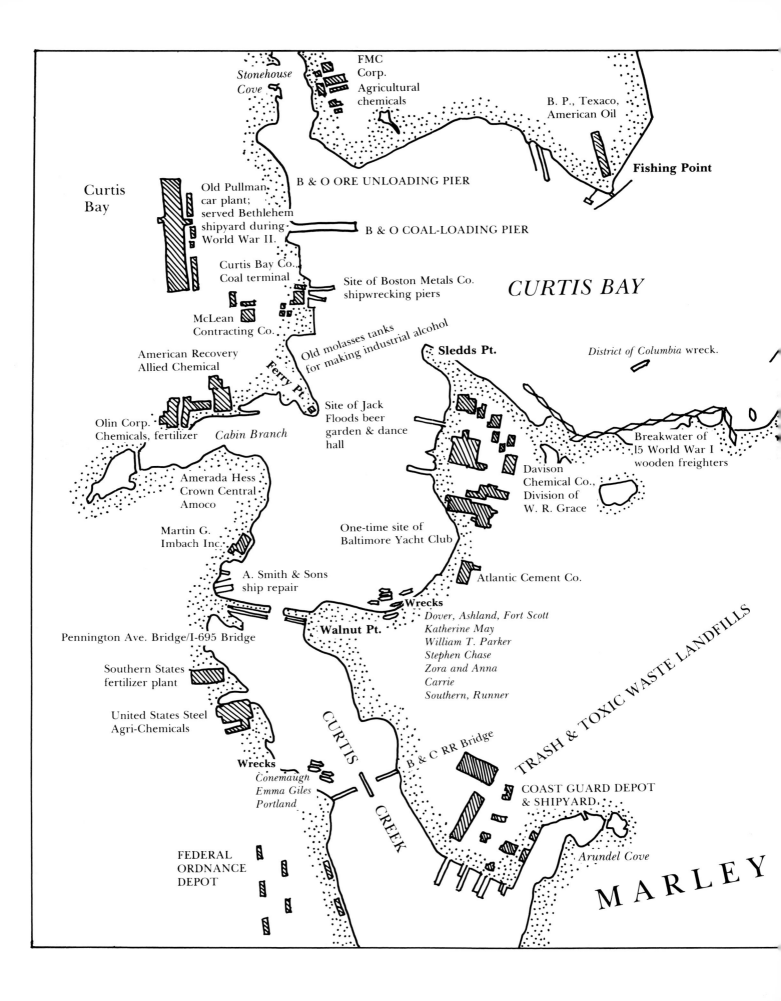

Stonehouse
Cove

FMC
Corp.
Agricultural
chemicals

B. P., Texaco,
American Oil

Fishing Point

Curtis
Bay

Old Pullman
car plant;
served Bethlehem
shipyard during
World War II.

B & O ORE UNLOADING PIER

B & O COAL-LOADING PIER

Curtis Bay Co.
Coal terminal

Site of Boston Metals Co.
shipwrecking piers

CURTIS BAY

McLean
Contracting Co.

Old molasses tanks
for making industrial alcohol

Sledds Pt.

District of Columbia wreck.

American Recovery
Allied Chemical

Ferry Pt.

Site of Jack
Floods beer
garden & dance
hall

Olin Corp.
Chemicals, fertilizer

Cabin Branch

Davison
Chemical Co.,
Division of
W. R. Grace

Breakwater of
15 World War I
wooden freighters

Amerada Hess
Crown Central
Amoco

Martin G.
Imbach Inc.

One-time site of
Baltimore Yacht Club

A. Smith & Sons
ship repair

Atlantic Cement Co.

Wrecks

Pennington Ave. Bridge/I-695 Bridge

Walnut Pt.

*Dover, Ashland, Fort Scott
Katherine May
William T. Parker
Stephen Chase
Zora and Anna
Carrie
Southern, Runner*

Southern States
fertilizer plant

United States Steel
Agri-Chemicals

TRASH & TOXIC WASTE LANDFILLS

Wrecks

*Conemaugh
Emma Giles
Portland*

CURTIS

CREEK

B & C RR Bridge

**COAST GUARD DEPOT
& SHIPYARD**

**FEDERAL
ORDNANCE
DEPOT**

Arundel Cove

M A R L E Y

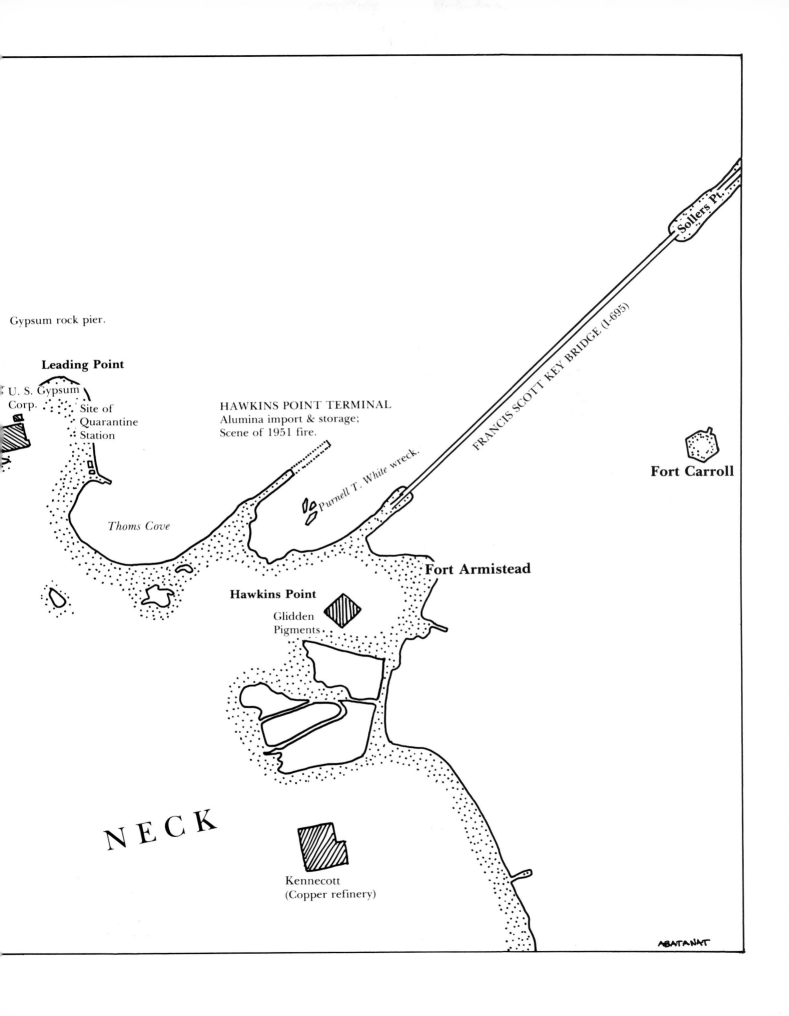

Gypsum rock pier.

Leading Point

U. S. Gypsum
Corp.

Site of
Quarantine
Station

Thoms Cove

HAWKINS POINT TERMINAL
Alumina import & storage;
Scene of 1951 fire.

Purnell T. White wreck.

Fort Armistead

Hawkins Point

Glidden
Pigments

FRANCIS SCOTT KEY BRIDGE (I-695)

Sollers Pt.

Fort Carroll

N E C K

Kennecott
(Copper refinery)

ABATANAT

Chapter 5

Curtis Bay Memories

BLANCHARD'S *A Cruising Guide to the Chesapeake* carries a warning about Curtis Creek: "Yachtsmen should stay out . . . The creek is very commercial, dirty and unattractive."

And so it is. But it is also one of the most interesting stretches of water on Chesapeake Bay.

Chemical plants abound, devoted particularly to the production of farm chemicals and fertilizer.

Oil tank "farms" can be seen everywhere, storing the supplies of fuel oil and gasoline for much of Maryland after they are brought by ship or pipeline.

Many will recall the 1982 air photos of coal freighters lying off Annapolis, awaiting a berth at Baltimore. Their destination was the Curtis Bay loading dock of the Baltimore & Ohio Railroad, at one time the largest in the world. Here giant cylindrical contraptions overturn coal cars from Appalachia one or two at at time and shake out their contents onto conveyor belts that feed the holds of each ship in turn, at a rate of 6,000 tons an hour.

Barges are loaded on the north side of the pier at an additional 4,000 tons an hour. Nearby are the eight futuristic conveyor towers and new coal pier of the Curtis Bay Co., an Occidental Petroleum subsidiary. The purpose of the towers is to distribute incoming coal in storage piles, so that the required type and grade will be immediately available for each awaiting ship.

Most of the coal exported here goes to Europe. From the same spot 75 years ago, five-, six-, and even one seven-masted schooner picked up cargoes of coal for the textile mills of New England.

The new coal pier replaced two old ship-breaking piers of the Boston Metals Co., which closed its salvage operations here in August, 1979. Chesapeake Bay steamboats, warships and steel freighters met their doom at the Boston Metals docks, which were in operation for more than a half century.

Ferry Point is a reminder of a bygone era, when Jack Flood's beer park on this spot lured Bal-

A coal freighter opens its hatch covers to receive cargo at the B & O loading pier on Curtis Bay . . . . In the foreground are the Curtis Bay Co.'s new coal stacking towers. The overhead conveyors carry the coal to the towers from railcars, with different grades directed to different storage areas. As the coal leaves the conveyor, it falls out of windows in the towers and stacks up around them in huge cones. When coal is needed to load a ship, it drops through or is pushed by bulldozer to an opening in the ground. Underground conveyors transport it to the loading dock. The B & O's ore unloading dock is marked by two large cranes at far left.

AUBREY PATTERSON

timoreans to Curtis Creek by the thousands, many coming by trolley across the old Light Street Bridge. Thirty showgirls awaited them, performing burlesque in white tights, then sitting with the customers and earning a 2 ½ cent commission on every 15 cent drink they "sold." The grounds had big shade trees, large open pavilions, picnic-type tables, a theater, and up to 125 waiters in long white aprons running back and forth with orders. Flood's served liquor on Sundays, which was the cause of its demise. "This brought the Billy Sunday crew, the Anti-Saloon League, the Home Defenders, and the Lord's Day Alliance down on him," a former employee reported. In 1916 Flood's license was not renewed and the days of his "Curtis Bay Park" were over.

Upstream from Ferry Point, past three bridges, is the only shipyard of the United States Coast Guard, established here in 1899, when Curtis Bay was lined with peach orchards and the waters abounded in trout, perch and rock. Repair and overhaul work on all Coast Guard vessels on the Gulf and Atlantic coasts is performed here; the three-masted training bark *Eagle* arrives for refitting every winter. The shipyard, with some 1,000 military and civilian employees, builds large cutters and makes all the channel marker buoys for United States coastal waters.

Across the Creek to the west is a giant government supply and stockpile depot, once operated by the Army but now under the jurisdiction of the General Services Administration.

Further upstream is tree-lined Marley Creek, which has seen no commercial traffic for several decades, not since the last of the watermelon boats made secret visits to pick up truckloads of their product and take them to the downtown public wharves, giving the appearance of bringing in an authentic cargo from the lower Bay. Branching off to the west is Furnace Creek, where an old foundry made cannonballs during the Revolutionary War.

Pennington Ave., I-695 bridges

A. Smith & Sons ship repair

Olin Corp.

Hess oil storage

Carrie   Cement boat   *Dover*   Ocean tug   *Ashland*
Zora and Anna   *Stephen Chase*
William T. Parker   Barges

This stone house on the Davison Chemical property overlooked Stansbury Cove from 1734 until it was demolished in 1956. It was located on the site of the first cabin built by Tobias Stansbury about 1636.

WILLIS SMITH COLLECTION

B & O ore pier

Curtis Bay Terminal/B & O coal pier

Davison Chemical

Ferry Point   Fairfield

Fort Scott

PHOTO BY AUTHOR

Gambler's yacht   Barge

Abandoned Ships

A VISITOR to Curtis Creek will find fascination at every hand, not only because of the great commercial installations, but because it is a graveyard of abandoned ships. The cluster shown above is at Stansbury Cove, next to the Pennington Ave. bridge. This cove was the earliest stopping point for European vessels on the Patapsco River, because of nearby artesian water supplies. (Heavy use of underground water by the Davison Chemical Co. has stopped the flow in the present century.) A British captain named Curtis brought ships here for water in the mid-1600s, which is apparently how the bay got its name.

Most of the ships left to disintegrate in this historic cove can be identified.* The one intact hull on the left is that of a ferro-cement steamer built for the Army during World War I, when the technique was developed. The wreckage along the beach at the left of the ferro-cement boat includes the rem-

nants of the schooners *William T. Parker, Zora and Anna,* and *Carrie.* To the right of the concrete hull, facing in opposite directions, are the hulks of two large wooden vessels built during World War I, the *Dover* and *Ashland.* Peering out just behind the stem of the *Ashland* can be seen the hawsepipe of a World War II ocean rescue tug. The crumbling remains at right of the picture are those of the World War I freighter *Fort Scott,* built in Oregon. Toward the camera from the facing rudders of the *Dover* and *Fort Scott* are the jutting ribs of the schooner *Stephen Chase,* built in Dorchester County, Maryland, in 1878. Barely visible alongside the *Fort Scott* are remains of a gambler's yacht. Right of that is an abandoned barge. The two huge hulks in the immediate foreground are believed to be old barges. Not visible in this picture are remains of the four-masted schooner *Katherine May,* behind the *Dover,* and the tugs *Runner* and *Southern,* near the *Fort Scott.*

More abandoned hulks lie beyond the bridge to the left, and further out the bay to the right, past the chemical plant. Each has a story to tell. Listen!

*Author and former Baltimorean Robert H. Burgess kept track of the Curtis Bay wrecks and is the source of much of the information here.

City of Norfolk's elegant interior. *Sunpapers* photo by A. Aubrey Bodine.

Curtis Bay Memories

Night Boat

On the night of April 13, 1962, the *City of Norfolk* blew one long blast upon leaving her slip, just as ships of the Baltimore Steam Packet Company had been doing since 1840. The sound of the whistle reverberated about Norfolk harbor, as it had always done. The *City of Norfolk* moved out into the channel, her electric lights etching her white cabins against the dark and stormy night. Her lovely sheer made her graceful from every angle as she turned her stern to Norfolk and disappeared into the rain. It was a sight that Norfolk had seen on thousands of occasions, but one it would never see again. The last American night boat was making her final sailing...When the *City of Norfolk* tied up in Baltimore the following morning, a characteristic American institution was ended, finally, inexorably and irrevocably. The night boat was an extinct form of transportation.*

FOR a century, from the mid-1800s to the mid-1900s, the "night boat" was an established part of the American transportation system, carrying passengers and freight between cities a few hundred miles apart: Baltimore and Norfolk, Washington, D.C., and Norfolk, Detroit and Cleveland, Detroit

The Night Boat by George W. Hilton. Copyright 1968 by Howell-North Books. All rights reserved.

and Buffalo, New York and Albany, New York and Boston. Typically, the night boats were paddle-wheel steamers, or resembled the paddle-wheelers in profile: wooden superstructure built out from the hull on overhanging guards, giving a beamy and comfortable appearance. George Hilton describes their attraction: "A leisurely dinner at prices comparable to restaurants on shore, a relaxed evening on deck or in the grand saloon, and a night of sleep in the creaking comfort of a berth afloat . . . " The price was an amazing bargain. Even at the end, when the company decided to abandon operations, the basic fare between Baltimore and Norfolk was only $5.50, with cabin charges ranging between $2 and $6.25.

The *City of Norfolk* and her companion ship, the *City of Richmond*, provided the last night boat service. The *Norfolk* was subsequently scrapped, being struck by lightning and catching fire in the process, and the *Richmond* was lost while being towed to the Caribbean in 1964, so they were not the last of their breed in existence. That distinction goes to the *District of Columbia*, which served the Baltimore-Norfolk run as a relief boat. The *District of Columbia* was built in 1925 for the Washington-Norfolk run, down the Potomac River. In 1948, off Old Point Comfort, it collided with the tanker *Georgia* and suffered heavy damage.

The Baltimore Steam Packet Co. (also known as the "Old Bay Line") bought the vessel, repaired it,

District of Columbia

R. LOREN GRAHAM

Afire at Pratt St. pier, 1969.

SUNPAPERS

and kept it operating out of Washington, D.C., until 1957. The ship was then brought to Baltimore as a backup to the *City of Richmond* and *City of Norfolk*. When those vessels ended their service in April 1962, the *District of Columbia* was taken to Cape Cod, renamed *Provincetown,* and employed as a cruise ferry between Boston and Provincetown during the 1962-63 summer seasons. The ship was purchased by Charles Hoffberger and returned to Baltimore in 1964. Hoffberger's plan was to restore her to operation in 1965, under the name *Chesapeake,* making two trips weekly from Wash-

ington, D.C. to Yorktown and Norfolk. But Coast Guard safety requirements proved too costly, and the plan was abandoned. Fire swept her upper decks in 1969 as she lay at her downtown Baltimore pier, dashing hopes of turning her into a restaurant. City authorities had the derelict towed to Curtis Bay in 1970. The following January she flooded and sank. A decade later there was talk of dynamiting her submerged hulk and taking the scrap. Meanwhile she lay on the bottom, her exposed smokestack and air funnels arousing the curiosity of passing vessels—America's last night boat.

District of Columbia, view of interior.

In Curtis Bay, 1982.   PHOTO BY AUTHOR

LEFT: Launching of one of the World War I wooden hulls at Baltimore, 1917-18. BELOW: Bow of *Dover*, a remnant of this building program, at Curtis Creek, 1982.

PEALE MUSEUM   PHOTO BY AUTHOR

Curtis Bay Memories

World War I Steamers

THE biggest and strangest of the Curtis Bay hulks are the remains of wooden freight steamers built during World War I. The freighters are the product of one of the least successful shipbuilding programs ever undertaken in this country. The United States Shipping Board proposed to build 800 to 1,000 of the 3,500 deadweight-ton ships within a period of 18 to 24 months, in order to keep ahead of the losses of American tonnage to German submarines. In the winter of 1917-1918 a "river of wood" flowed by railroad from Oregon to Atlantic and Gulf shipyards, bringing heavy lumber for hull construction. Only a small portion of the ships were delivered before the Armistice of Nov. 11, 1918. However, this was a government project that took on a life of its own, and the building of the ships continued even though the circumstances which led to their construction had ceased to exist. Other than for meeting a wartime emergency, the ships had no value whatsoever. They lacked the stamina of steel vessels in carrying pro-

pulsion machinery and bucking heavy seas. They were too small to operate economically on long voyages, yet generally too large and heavy to be used successfully as barges. They were built hastily of green timber and not properly caulked. Complained one irate skipper, referring to the materials used in his ship, "They sent out oak shoots in April and provided pine cones for the Christmas mess." In September 1925, 200 of the wooden steamers, built at a cost of $1 million apiece, were burned to the waterline at Mallows Bay in the Potomac River, across from Quantico, Virginia, for scrap metal.

In Baltimore, 15 of the hulks were sunk end to end along the southeast shore of Curtis Bay to make a breakwater, still visible. Three others, the *Dover, Ashland* and *Fort Scott* were acquired by the Davison Chemical Co. about 1919 and used as barges to bring pyrite ore from Cuba. They were abandoned in Curtis Creek in 1923. Their superstructures still loom out of the mud to puzzle the occupants of passing cars on a nearby freeway.

Curtis Bay Memories

The Schooners

O F ALL the vessel types represented in the Curtis Bay graveyard, none played a more important part in Chesapeake Bay commerce than the great old cargo schooners. Designed to operate with a minimum of crew, these wooden ships were a common sight in Baltimore harbor, transporting oysters, lumber, coal and other bulk materials, as well as general cargo. A hundred of them were operating as recently as 1930.

The identities and lives of the Curtis Bay schooners were chronicled by Robert Burgess, and their vital statistics are recorded in *Merchant Vessels of the United States,* annual volumes. Here is a thumbnail rundown:

PURNELL T. WHITE. Four-masted schooner. Built Sharptown, Maryland, 1917. Dismasted at sea, 1934; towed to Norfolk, then Baltimore with intentions of converting into barge; left to rot off Locust Point. Landfill was dumped over the hull, the decks fell in and   set fire to the bow. In 1957 a massive dredging and clearance project was undertaken at Locust Point to make way for a fruit terminal. Astonishingly, the *White* was refloated and towed to Hawkins Point, where her remains are no longer identifiable.

KATHERINE MAY. Four-masted schooner. Built 1919 in Maine for $175,000. Came to Baltimore in 1931 from Bermuda, under British registry. Couldn't find cargo during depression, eventually filled and sank at a pier near Federal Hill; was auctioned off for $405, raised, towed to Curtis Creek and abandoned.

WILLIAM T. PARKER. Three-masted schooner. Built Milton, Delaware, 1891. Lumber carrier. Stranded off Cape Henlopen Aug. 27, 1899; repaired. Disabled in gale off North Carolina Sept. 10, 1908. Abandoned in severe storm off Carolinas about 1915, drifted to Maine and back down coast, towed to port and reconditioned. Topmasts removed about 1929. Rammed off Bloody Point in Chesapeake Bay Feb. 24, 1935 by steamer *Commercial Bostonian;* sailed to Annapolis for anchorage, then to Marley Creek where lumber cargo was unloaded and A. Smith & Sons surveyed

Four-masted schooner *Katherine May* laid up off Locust Point sugar refinery in the 1930s. Photo by A. Aubrey Bodine.

Centerboard well of *Zora and Anna,* 1981.
JERRY SMITH

Remains of William T. Parker, 1981.
JERRY SMITH

PHOTO BY AUTHOR

Katherine May in 1982, at right of picture, turning back into a tree.

damage. Upon determination that repairs would be too costly, the *Parker* was towed to Locust Point where it was used for seven years as a home. It was moved to Curtis Creek in 1945. A watchman, Jake Bluhm, and his wife lived aboard the hulk for several years, until a steamer broke loose from its tug one night and crashed into the *Parker,* nearly breaking it in two.

ZORA AND ANNA. Schooner. Built 1855 as *Ocean Bird,* making her oldest known wreck in Curtis Bay; rebuilt as *Zora and Anna* at Sharptown, Maryland, 1910. 86 gross tons, 83.8 feet long, 23.8 feet wide, 6.3 feet deep. Owner Joseph E. Elliott, home port Annapolis. Abandoned 1941.

CARRIE. Centerboard schooner. 93 feet long, 23 feet wide, 6.6 feet deep. Built 1882, Cambridge, Maryland.

STEPHEN CHASE. Centerboard schooner. Built Dorchester County, Maryland, 1876. 66.6 feet long, 23.9 feet wide, 6.7 feet deep. About 1939 Capt. Major Todd sold to a relative, Emmet Carew of Brooklyn, Maryland. Was moored next to *Katherine May* and someone lived aboard. Then was moved to inner side of *Dover,* filled and sank. Listed abandoned 1946.

H. K. PRICE. Schooner. Beached at A. Smith & Sons yard in 1933. Had intended to convert to power but found hull was too weak. Destroyed when new bridge was constructed over Curtis Creek.

HANNA AND IDA. Schooner. Broke off masts going under bridge on Chesapeake & Delaware canal in 1935. Hull towed to Marley Creek for use as breakwater. Exact location unknown.

LEFT: Schooner *Purnell T. White* at Woodall yard, 1931. The *White* was regarded as the handsomest of the large schooners that visited Baltimore in this century. The graceful sheer of her deckline is very evident here.

BELOW: A schooner carrying a cargo of rock,

The *Emma Giles'* hull was taken for scrap in 1959 . . . . Emma Giles Parker, the company director's daughter who had christened her, died the same year at age 81.

LAURA F.BROWN

Curtis Bay Memories

Emma Giles

OF ALL the sidewheel passenger steamers to operate out of Baltimore, none was better known or more popular than the *Emma Giles*, built in 1887 for the Tolchester Co. For nearly a half century she carried weekend excursionists from the Inner Harbor to the beaches across the Bay at Tolchester, and on weekdays moved passengers and cargo to other points along the Bay: Port Deposit, Annapolis, West River, Little Choptank. A scene of a beehive with bees hovering over flowering plants was carved on her paddle boxes, along with the legend, "She was as busy as the bee."

At the close of the 1936 season the Tolchester operation was suspended and the *Emma Giles* was sold. Two years later she was taken to the place where she was built, the former William E. Woodall shipyard at Locust Point, and converted to a barge. For about ten years she brought lumber to Baltimore from points in North Carolina, her owner Capt. George F. Curlett, boasting that she could carry more lumber than any other barge working the inland waterway.

When this trade ended she was taken by a Baltimore shipbreaker to mudflats at the mouth of Curtis Bay, where she served for another ten years or so as a bulkhead, surrounded with dirt. Then the site was needed for a new ore pier and all the hulks in the area, including that of the *Giles*, had

45

to be removed. She was cleared of dirt and re-floated, and towed up Curtis Creek beyond the Pennington Avenue bridge. Then she was set on fire, in an effort to expose her iron frames for scrap. A portion of her charred stern remained visible for a number of years.

It seemed strange to look at that lifeless wreckage, and then recall a passage from the Barrie brothers book, describing the arrival of the *Emma Giles* in Annapolis around the turn of the century:*

About half-past ten o'clock the steamer will be seen coming from behind Greenberry Point, and as she passes the light-house gives a long blast from her whistle. Then the "tailor" fishers lift up their rods and gather up their paraphernalia, swing in their legs, and stand among the curious crowd which has gathered, the larger portion

*Robert Barrie and George Barrie, Jr., *Cruises, Mainly on the Bay of the Chesapeake*, The Franklin Press, 1909.

being small boys, both white and black; the town loafers, and perhaps a few prospective passengers. In the background are half a dozen hacks, in most of which Washington rode the day he resigned his commission, and eight or ten wagons awaiting for the freight. In a few minutes she is along-side the wharf, the captain being a master hand at this; over the rails leans a crowd of women and children, the latter in such abundance that one is firmly convinced that all of the youngsters and babies of Baltimore are on an outing. Just as the lines are fast a laggardly hack or wagon will clatter down the vitrified brick street at full gallop, the horses covered with lather and the driver cracking his whip and yelling at the top of his voice to the gapping crowd; suddenly he pulls up, the horses sliding and the pole almost sticking into the barouche ahead. When the gang-plank is on the wharf, first off are passengers; a drummer or two, and a few people who have come on a visit, but the majority are "trippers," who, while the steamer re-

Stevedores transferring cargo from a Chesapeake Bay steamer.

H. Graham Wood

mains, walk to the Academy. Then comes another gang-plank and pandemonium breaks loose in the form of fifteen (black stevedores) clad in the tatters of shirt, trousers, and shoes. They have been lined up on the main deck, each man with a truck in front of him loaded to its utmost; down one plank they tear; up into the freight house, which is soon filled; dump, and back on board by the other plank. They keep this up continuously even on the hottest of sultry August days, singing, shouting, and doing fancy steps, always in good humor, although they are pestered by small children getting in the way, and there are some narrow escapes, but the stevedore makes a quick turn or a short stop and the stray youngster is hauled off by a chattering parent . . . In the meantime, crates of vegetables, boxes of shoes, pieces of farming implements, sides of beef, even barrels of moulder's sand, window-frames, sofas, bags of flour or meal, which often-times leaves a trail along the deck and into the shed, boxes of canned goods, now and then a barrel of crab-bait , from which a thousand flies have been disturbed, is trundled off, leaving a reeking trail along which the persistent flies are buzzing like a pack of hounds on a fox's scent, coils of rope for the ship-chandlers on the city dock, plumbers supplies; in fact, boxes and bundles of every conceivable size and shape containing all sorts of articles . . . are soon scattered over the wharf.

When nearly all are off a few shipments for the landings on West River are taken on, then the trucks are stacked and a carriage or cart followed by a horse is run off; the whistle blows, the last tripper dashes down and jumps on board just as the lines are cast off and the *Giles* backs off into the harbor, leaving a trail of froth dotted here and there by a shoe-box which contained some delicatessen.

By this time the hacks that were fortunate enough to get a fare have long since swayed off up the street and the others are now straggling off; the wagons are loading and soon they have disappeared; the loafers are gone; the anglers are once more absorbed in catching the tooth-some "tailor"; the agent is sitting in the doorway of the freight shed to catch the breeze, his pocket handkerchief in one hand mopping his red face and fanning with his hat in the other. The usual reign of quiet being broken only by the occasional bleat of the small brown veal in the cattle-pen waiting to be taken to Baltimore when the steamer stops on her return trip in the afternoon.

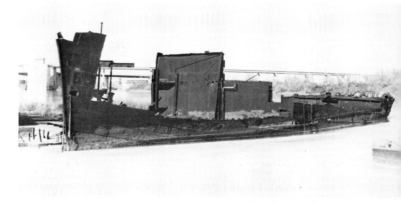

PHOTO BY AUTHOR

Conemaugh

ONE of the biggest hulks in Curtis Bay, and at one time the handsomest, is the 260-foot iron-hulled *Conemaugh*. She was built by T. Royden & Sons at Liverpool, England, in 1879 as the square-rigged *Lortney*, a crack sailer of her time, according to Robert Burgess.* In 1885 she was damaged in collision and classified a total loss. Two years later she reappeared as the four-masted schooner *Atlas*, registered in Boston, and carrying just enough sail to aid a tug in favorable winds.

According to Burgess, she carried coal, crushed stone and fruit before being converted in 1902 to an oil barge and renamed *Conemaugh*. She carried oil out of Texas ports until the late 1930s, when she appeared in Baltimore as a storage hulk for ships about to be scrapped by the Union Shipbuilding Co. at Fairfield. At the start of World War II she was towed to Locust Point and abandoned, and dirt filled in over her port side. In 1951 a scrap dealer obtained title to her, patched her and pumped her out—obtaining a substantial cargo of fuel oil in the process—and towed her to Curtis Bay. Here her sides were stripped away, leaving only a desolate reminder of her once-graceful frame.

In November 1982, wrecking barges gathered alongside the forlorn ruin, and began pecking away at the last scraps. The dismantling of the *Conemaugh* was part of a cleanup effort that also resulted in removal of some of the barges shown on the following page.

*Robert H. Burgess, *Chesapeake Circle*, Cornell Maritime Press, 1965, p. 18

These old hulks, many of them unidentified, slowly disintegrate at an old shipbreakers yard on Curtis Creek
above Pennington Ave. bridge. The rounded objects at
far left are forms for making circular steel caissons in
marine construction projects.

A bit further up Curtis Creek is the yard and depot of
the U. S. Coast Guard. This is how the yard looked after
it was established on Arundel Cove at the turn of the
century. The yard grew as the Lifesaving Service was
combined with the Revenue Cutter Service in 1915 to
form the Coast Guard; the Lighthouse Service was added
in 1939. Additional shipways, shops and piers were built
soon after the outbreak of World War II.

PHOTO BY AUTHOR

BALTIMORE GAS & ELECTRIC CO.

Chapter 6

Miracle at Fairfield

WEST of Curtis Bay, past the Patapsco Sewage Treatment Plant at Wagner's Point and also beyond an assortment of oil unloading docks, on a wide fist of land known as Fairfield and at the exact spot where a highway tunnel plunges below the ground, lies the most amazing industrial site in Baltimore harbor. This is the place where Bethlehem Steel Corp. built 508 steel ships during World War II.

The yard was established by the Union Shipbuilding Co. in World War I. Union turned to shipbreaking in the mid 1920s. Among its victims: the *Morro Castle,* purchased for $39,000 and towed to the yard for scrapping after it was swept by fire off the Jersey Coast in 1934 with a loss of 134 lives.

With a government order for 50 ships—first of the famed Liberty ships—Bethlehem leased the Union yard in 1941, added 12 ship ways to the four already there, and took over the 33-acre Pullman & Standard Steel Co. plant two miles to the south along the B & O Railroad line. The heavy duty machinery of the Pullman plant—which turned out 25 railroad cars a day in its heyday–was rearranged into a mass production line for ship components. The components were brought to the shipyard by B & O and assembled on the ways.

The keel for the first ship, the *Patrick Henry,* was laid April 30, 1941. The ship was launched Sept. 27 and delivered Dec. 30. By the time the yard reached peak round-the-clock production, it em-

After launching, Liberty ships were towed to this pier to be completed and fitted out for sea. *Sunpapers* photo by A. Aubrey Bodine.

ployed 47,000 persons and brought the time between keel-laying and launch to less than 30 days (19 days was the record). There was a time when a ship was coming down the ways every 24 hours. After building 384 Liberty ships—a line of ships 32 miles long—the yard switched in 1944 to "Victory" ships, faster and more suitable for postwar commerce. It built 94 of these along with 30 landing craft. In a grand finale, the yard conducted a triple launch of Victory ships between Sept. 19 and 22, 1945, shortly after war's end, and went out of business.

In a space of less than five years, Bethlehem's Fairfield yard built 5,187,800 tons of shipping, 10 percent of the American fleet, and more tonnage and more ships than any other of the wartime mass production yards. The company attested to an aftertax profit of $14.2 million on the operation, about $28,000 per ship built.

In 1946, Bethlehem, which by then owned the property, established the Patapsco Scrap Corp. to undo what had been done and feed the blast furnaces of Sparrows Point and other Bethlehem plants. Many Liberty ships came back to die at the place where they were born, including the *Patrick Henry*. After a successful career under the operation of Lykes Steamship Lines of New Orleans, the *Patrick Henry* was retired to the reserve fleet in Mobile River, Alabama, on Aug. 28, 1946 needing a $75,000 overhaul. A move to persuade the Pro-

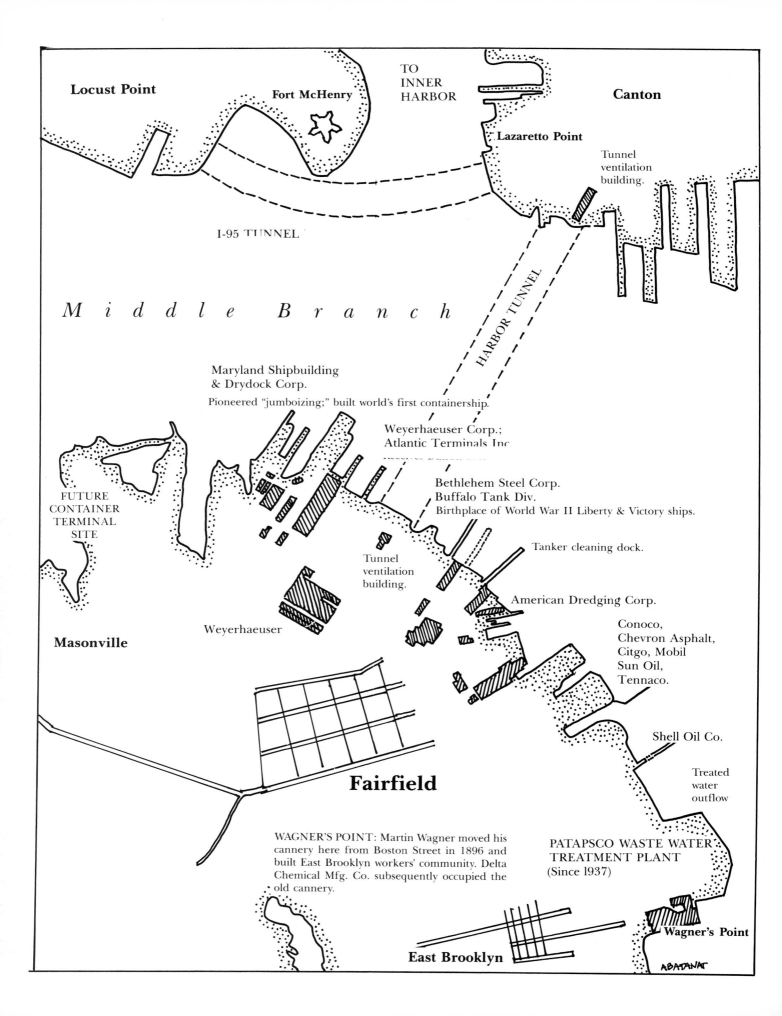

Locust Point

Fort McHenry

TO
INNER
HARBOR

Canton

Lazaretto Point

Tunnel
ventilation
building.

I-95 TUNNEL

M i d d l e   B r a n c h

HARBOR TUNNEL

Maryland Shipbuilding
& Drydock Corp.

Pioneered "jumboizing;" built world's first containership.

Weyerhaeuser Corp.;
Atlantic Terminals Inc.

FUTURE
CONTAINER
TERMINAL
SITE

Bethlehem Steel Corp.
Buffalo Tank Div.

Birthplace of World War II Liberty & Victory ships.

Tanker cleaning dock.

Tunnel
ventilation
building.

American Dredging Corp.

Masonville

Weyerhaeuser

Conoco,
Chevron Asphalt,
Citgo, Mobil
Sun Oil,
Tennaco.

Shell Oil Co.

Treated
water
outflow

Fairfield

WAGNER'S POINT: Martin Wagner moved his
cannery here from Boston Street in 1896 and
built East Brooklyn workers' community. Delta
Chemical Mfg. Co. subsequently occupied the
old cannery.

PATAPSCO WASTE WATER
TREATMENT PLANT
(Since 1937)

Wagner's Point

East Brooklyn

ABATANAT

peller Club of Baltimore to preserve the ship as a symbol of the American merchant marine failed; she was returned to the Fairfield site for scrapping on Oct. 26, 1958.

Early in 1960, after the Government decided to sell many old Liberty ships from the reserve fleets, more than 100 of the vessels were tied up in Curtis Bay awaiting their fate. The Patapsco Scrap yard subdued many of these as well as several battleships before closing down June 30, 1964. Bethlehem offered it for sale for $2.6 million but found no takers. Today it is used by Bethlehem's Buffalo Tank Division, making all sizes and shapes of steel storage tanks, pressure tanks and platework, primarily for the chemical and petroleum industries. One of the docks is equipped for the steam-cleaning of oil tankers, which must be done before these ships enter a repair yard or take on a different type of cargo, such as grain. (The cleaning operations were suspended in 1982 because of Environmental Protection Agency regulations and lack of demand; many ships are able to clean themselves at sea.)

Some 15 companies lease space in the old six-block long Pullman plant, which forms the eastern boundary of the town of Curtis Bay.

PEALE MUSEUM

Launching of the *Patrick Henry,* Sept. 27, 1941 . . . . Called the "ugly ducklings of the sea lanes," the Liberty ships were 441 feet 7 ½ inches long, 56 feet 10 ¾ inches wide and carried 10,500 tons of cargo in their five big holds. Their oil-buring steam reciprocating engine moved them at a speed of 11 knots. They cost about $1.9 million apiece to build . . . . The later Victory ships moved at 15 knots with high pressure steam turbines and cost about $2,250,000 apiece. Photo below shows Victory ships being fitted out at Fairfield in 1945.

PEALE MUSEUM

WEST of the old Bethlehem yard, beyond the old Weyerhaeuser lumber pier (which was used in recent times for the landing of autos from Japan) are the remains of another harbor institution, the Maryland Shipbuilding and Drydock Co. This was started in 1920 as the Maryland Drydock Co. when Baltimore financial interests purchased the Globe Shipbuilding Co. in Superior, Wisconsin, and moved it to the initial 70-acre tract at Fairfield.

The yard became known as a place where damaged or seaworn ships were doctored and returned to service, or converted to some new purpose. The yard pioneered the technique of "jumboizing"— cutting a ship in half, separating the two sections, and welding a new section in the middle to increase capacity. During World War II the yard was enlarged to provide berths for 31 ships; "Shipbuilding" was added to the title in 1955. In January 1960 the yard converted the Grace Line freighter *Santa Eliana* to a containership by adding side blisters or "sponsons" to make it wider; on June 14 of the same year it launched the world's first completely new containership, the MV *Floridian*, for use by the Erie & St. Lawrence Corp. between New York City and Jacksonville. In 1967, the Fruehauf Corp. of Detroit, the trailer-maker. took over the yard from Koppers' Corp. through an exchange of stock. Fruehauf undertook a $30 million expansion program in 1974. The yard was beset with a series of labor disputes, along with mounting competition from abroad. In July 1984, with business at a standstill, Fruehauf closed the yard.

Idle ships tied off Maryland Shipbuilding & Drydock, June 1958.

MARYLAND HISTORICAL SOCIETY

BALTIMORE GAS & ELECTRIC CO.

This air view, looking southeast, shows Fairfield in the mid-1960s, with the Maryland Shipbuilding & Drydock Co. in foreground . . . . The Weyerhaeuser pier and buildings are immediately behind the shipyard. The Harbor Tunnel Thruway bisects the picture and disappears beneath the ventilation building at left center. Remains of the Bethlehem World War II shipyard can be seen beyond the ventilation building. Beyond the Thruway, the communities of Fairfield (upper right) and East Brooklyn (upper center) are barely distinguishable in a sea of oil and gas tanks. Curtis Creek is at top of photo, with the B & O coal and ore piers visible beyond Stonehouse Cove at upper right.

PEALE MUSEUM

Launching of the *Floridian.* the first containership, at Maryland Shipbuilding and Drydock, 1960.

Chapter 7

Middle Branch

AS YOU travel west from Fairfield and Fort McHenry, toward the Hanover Street Bridge, you are moving away from the Baltimore that is, to the Baltimore that might have been. The founders of Baltimore Town proposed to locate their community here, on the "Middle Branch" of the Patapsco, rather than at the shallow, swampy harbor to the north.

If they had succeeded, the landscape would surely be quite different from the view shown in this 1959 photo. In the foreground is the Port Covington terminal complex established by the Western Maryland Railroad in 1903 and now controlled by the Maryland Port Administration. The huge grain elevator, operated by the Connecticut-based Louis Dreyfus Corp., was built in 1929. Just beyond it is Ferry Bar point, one of Baltimore's most popular spots before the coming of industry and removal of the river crossing to Hanover Street to the west. In 1989 the grain elevator and the railyard north of it were erased by wrecking crews and the area was converted to a job-inducing industrial park.

MARYLAND HISTORICAL SOCIETY

The plan to put Baltimore on the Middle Branch was thwarted by John Moale, an English immigrant who arrived in 1719. Moale bought land on the north shore, in what is now called South Baltimore, and apparently also on the south shore, taking in the present Cherry Hill. Moale thought there was more money to be made in the mining of iron ore than in real estate speculation, so he prevailed on the colonial legislature in Annapolis to defeat a bill that would have created Baltimore Town on his own lands. Moale was influenced by the fact that the English-controlled Principio Furnace Co. was conducting mining operations on nearby Whetstone Point (now Locust Point) to feed its iron furnaces at the head of Chesapeake Bay. Stockholders of the company included Augustine and Lawrence Washington, father and brother of George. Ore was also being dug nearby by the Baltimore Co., which ran an iron furnace at the mouth of Gwynns Falls. This remained in operation until about the time of the Civil War.

Overshadowing the mining operations on the Middle Branch in those days was the shipping of tobacco and, a little later, the milling of flour. "Hogsheads" of tobacco were rolled down Rolling Road in Baltimore County (the road bears the same name today) to Elk Ridge Landing (now Elkridge) which in the mid-1700s had a customs house, a race track, and a deep channel leading to the open river (see page 16), making it Maryland's second

Rolling a hogshead of tobacco.

HARPER'S WEEKLY, 1869

port after Annapolis. In 1772, the Ellicott brothers built the country's largest flour mill further upstream (now Ellicott City). In 1830 this became the first destination of the horsedrawn Baltimore & Ohio Railroad.

A great flood on the Patapsco on July 24, 1868 ended the milling era. The raging waters destroyed a town (Avalon), engulfed a mail train, killed 50 persons and wiped out many of the mills. They were never rebuilt.

Winans cigar ship at sea, as envisioned by builder.

THE ILLUSTRATED LONDON NEWS—PEALE MUSEUM

MARYLAND HISTORICAL SOCIETY

Experimental Ships

IN 1869, the Baltimore lithography firm E. Sachse & Co. distributed this "bird's-eye view" showing Ferry Bar point and the pier and shipyard of the inventor-engineer Ross Winans and his son Thomas. The famous Winan's "cigar boat" is shown docked at the pier. Ross Winans came to Baltimore in the 1820s to build cars and locomotives at the Mount Clare shops of the Baltimore & Ohio Railroad. He helped Peter Cooper design the Tom Thumb (see page 130). Shortly before the Civil War, he bought land on both sides of the Middle Branch. The property on the west side came to be known as Mt. Winans. The property on the east side included Ferry Bar and the present Port Covington Terminal.

Turning his inventive mind to ships, Ross Winans conceived a hull design that he thought could cross the Atlantic in four days. The ship was built by Thomas Winans and launched in 1858. It was radical for its time, in that it was intended to master the open ocean by steam power alone. Freed of the need to support wind-filled sails, Winans reasoned, the hull could be made long, round and thin, and thus make a streamlined cut through the water. The resultant "cigar boat" was 180 feet long and 16 feet wide. It was propelled by an iron wheel with flanges, which circled the vessel at mid-ships and was driven by machinery from the inside. The ship attained a speed of 12 miles an hour on its first trial run in January, 1859, but any passenger taking a walk on the deck quickly discovered the flaw in Winans' design, and returned, drenched, to the stuffy confines of the ship. The Winans lengthened their vessel to 194 feet in February and to 235 feet in October. In November the craft went to Norfolk and made several experimental trips to sea. The Winans built three other cigar boats, one in Russia in 1861 and two in England in 1864 with conventional screw propulsion, but none was commercially successful. The first ship was returned to its Baltimore dock where it remained until it fell to pieces.

On June 10, 1876, Thomas Winans launched the *Sokoloff*, a 32-foot sailing yacht of which it was claimed she "will not upset in the strongest gale," despite a large press of canvas. The reason for the claimed stability was that the three-foot-deep iron keel was separated from the body of the boat and fastened to it by brass gudgeons fore and aft, so that the body could swing clear. The 36-foot mast was fastened to the keel at the bow. In a gust of wind the mast and keel would go over but the body would remain upright. Success of the the vessel is not recorded.

59

ENOCH PRATT PUBLIC LIBRARY

Boating and Beer Parks

A NUMBER of resorts sprang up on the Middle Branch in the late 1800s, most notably George Kahl's Ferry Bar. Here, during the "Gay Nineties," you could get a huge bowl of crab soup for a dime, and for 50 cents you could get a shore dinner consisting of half a fried chicken, a soft crab, farm-fresh vegetables from across the bridge in Anne Arundel County, french-fried potatoes, hot muffins, and all the coffee you could drink. An electric launch transported patrons to other resorts on the basin.

The area was a mecca for swimmers, fishermen and pleasure boaters. The Baltimore Yacht Club (now at Middle River) was located upstream from Ferry Bar point, while the Maryland Yacht Club (now at Rock Creek) established itself across the river to the south. Along the northeast shore were the Corinthian Yacht Club (active in Bear Creek until 1955), the Ariel Rowing Club, the Arundel Boat Club, the Baltimore Athletic Club and a branch of the Baltimore Public Baths. Informal swimming could be found on the south side, where a sand beach stretched all the way from Hanover Street to the Maryland Drydock Co.

Bathing beauties . . . . The rented suits at the Baltimore Public Baths reflected the modesty of the times— until they got wet.

MARYLAND HISTORICAL SOCIETY

Rowing competition . . . . The protected waters of the Middle Branch were ideal for sculling. The Ariel and Arundel rowing clubs competed with each other and with other mid-Atlantic clubs, and were known as "the Patapsco Navy." Above, Ariel club members practice alongside an unidentified four-masted schooner. Below, the Ariel team poses for a group portrait. The Ariel club was last heard from in 1927, but a revival of rowing was taking place in 1982 at Jackson's Wharf in Fells Point.

MARYLAND HISTORICAL SOCIETY

Bridging the River

THE first bridge over the Middle Branch was the wooden "long bridge" at Ferry Bar point, built in 1856. The bridge was an extension of Light Street, which ran to the river in those days, and then continued on for a number of miles in Anne Arundel County on the south side. The present ornate Hanover Street Bridge was built in 1914. The Corinthian Yacht Club docks can be seen on the far side in the construction photo at left, looking north. Below, the drawspans rise to accomodate a three-masted schooner making its way up the Middle Branch basin. To the immediate right of the bridge is the former Hanover Bridge Marina, now called Baltimore Yacht Basin. Next to it is Locke Insulator's porcelain manufacturing plant, one of the country's largest. Since 1974 the plant has been operated as a joint venture between General Electric Co. and N.G.K. Industries Ltd. of Japan, with N.G.K. holding 60 percent interest. The City of Baltimore continues to man the bridge around the clock though few vessels require the raising of its drawspans, except for a Coast Guard buoy tender that passes through perhaps once or twice a month.

MARYLAND
HISTORICAL
SOCIETY
PHOTOS

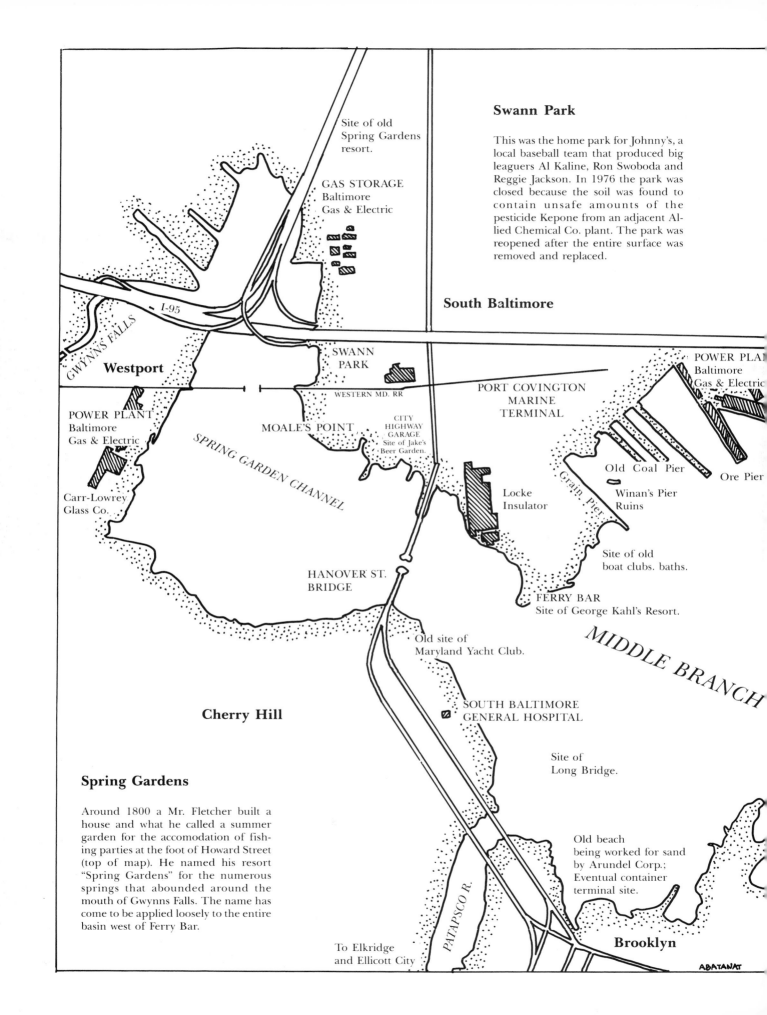

Swann Park

This was the home park for Johnny's, a local baseball team that produced big leaguers Al Kaline, Ron Swoboda and Reggie Jackson. In 1976 the park was closed because the soil was found to contain unsafe amounts of the pesticide Kepone from an adjacent Allied Chemical Co. plant. The park was reopened after the entire surface was removed and replaced.

South Baltimore

Site of old Spring Gardens resort.

GAS STORAGE
Baltimore Gas & Electric

I-95

GWYNNS FALLS

Westport

SWANN PARK

WESTERN MD. RR

POWER PLANT
Baltimore Gas & Electric

POWER PLANT
Baltimore Gas & Electric

Carr-Lowrey Glass Co.

MOALE'S POINT

CITY HIGHWAY GARAGE
Site of Jake's Beer Garden.

PORT COVINGTON MARINE TERMINAL

SPRING GARDEN CHANNEL

Locke Insulator

Grain Pier

Old Coal Pier

Winan's Pier Ruins

Ore Pier

Site of old boat clubs. baths.

HANOVER ST. BRIDGE

FERRY BAR
Site of George Kahl's Resort.

MIDDLE BRANCH

Old site of Maryland Yacht Club.

Cherry Hill

SOUTH BALTIMORE GENERAL HOSPITAL

Site of Long Bridge.

Spring Gardens

Around 1800 a Mr. Fletcher built a house and what he called a summer garden for the accomodation of fishing parties at the foot of Howard Street (top of map). He named his resort "Spring Gardens" for the numerous springs that abounded around the mouth of Gwynns Falls. The name has come to be applied loosely to the entire basin west of Ferry Bar.

Old beach being worked for sand by Arundel Corp.; Eventual container terminal site.

PATAPSCO R.

Brooklyn

To Elkridge and Ellicott City

ABATANAT

MARYLAND HISTORICAL SOCIETY PHOTOS

Pacific Mail Steamship Co. ships at Port Covington, April 1920 . . . . The two-masted boat at left is a Chesapeake Bay bugeye. The railroad cars in center are loading onto barges, which will be taken alongside the ships. The use of barges to supplement dockside loading and unloading speeded the handling of a ship in port, and eliminated the need to get the rail cars to the exact spot where the ship was moored.

Unloading ore . . . . The freighter *Andalusia* is unloaded at the Port Covington ore pier. The bucket can be seen as it is raised from the cargo hold. The ore is dropped in hoppers and fed into the waiting railroad cars.

Chapter 8

Locust Point

MARYLAND HISTORICAL SOCIETY

ALMOST everyone knows that Fort McHenry, at the tip of Locust Point, played an important role in American history. But how many are aware of the role played by the sprawling commercial establishment west of the fort? Here arose one of the largest railroad/sea terminal complexes on the face of the earth. The Locust Point terminal of the Baltimore & Ohio Railroad, on the north side of the   has been a vital instrument in the nation's export of coal and grain, and in the movement of general cargo, since its founding a century and a half ago. The Port Covington yards of the Western Maryland Railroad handled additional vast tonnages since their establishment in the early 1900s. Today both terminals are under the control of the Maryland Port Administration, and the facilities are geared to handle goods brought in by truck as well as train.

Through these terminals flow the goods of international commerce: tires, vehicles, spices, molasses, latex, almost everything imaginable that can be carried by ship.

Originally the tip of land now occupied by Fort McHenry was called Whetstone Point, and it was, in 1706, the second official Port of Entry recognized by Maryland's colonial legislature for ships entering the Patapsco River (Humphrey Creek, which now flows through the Sparrows Point steel

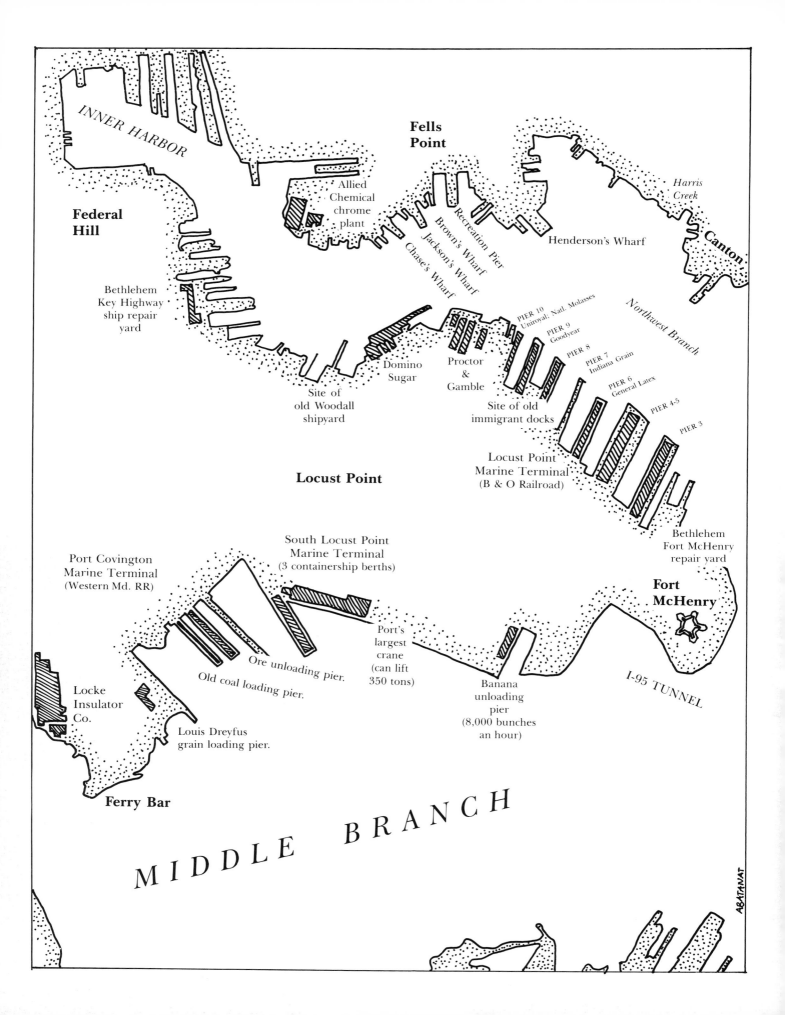

plant, was the first, in 1687). The only reason for an ocean vessel to call in those days was to pick up a cargo of tobacco.

Except for some iron mining by the Principio Furnace Co. in the 1700s, there was little activity on the point until 1845 when the B & O obtained permission to build its rail line to the water and establish an ocean terminal. At that time, Locust Point referred only to the protrusion of land now occupied by the Domino sugar and Proctor & Gamble soap plants. The first B & O facilities were located in this area. As the B & O complex expanded eastward, the entire peninsula came to be known as Locust Point, and the name was also taken by the workers' community which arose south of the rail yards.

B & O operated its Locust Point facility until 1964, when the MPA took it over (except for the grain terminal), radically improved truck access and reconstructed the piers, creating 17 modern berths. The pier 4-5 complex is now the largest general cargo pier in the port. MPA has a 40-year lease on the piers, while B & O continues to control the 3,750-car rail holding yard and maintains exclusive rail service to the terminal.

At South Locust Point, near Fort McHenry, the MPA put a new three-berth container terminal in service in 1979. It was placed just west of a banana dock where, from 1958 to 1981, the sleek white ships of United Brands could unload up to 8,000 bunches an hour. The dock was later torn down to make way for containers. Beyond the fort to the northwest, between the Naval Reserve station and the North Locust Point Terminal, is the drydock of the old Columbian Iron Works, later incorporated into Bethlehem Steel's Key Highway ship repair complex.

Rail cars at Locust Point, before pier reconstruction. Railroads dominated the port until the mid-1960s.

MARYLAND HISTORICAL SOCIETY

B & O's "Elevator C" put grain aboard ocean ships at Locust Point from 1891 until a spectacular fire destroyed it in 1922 . . . . Local news photographer Eugene McPhee caught the scene, below.

The Age of Sail persisted alongside the Age of Steam well into the present century . . . .
Here the freighter *Zitella* loads at Locust Point's present-day grain terminal, while a three-masted bark can be seen loading on the other side of the pier. The grain is conveyed overhead to the pier from an adjacent 3.8 million bushel storage elevator and fed down long chutes into the cargo hold. The barges at right in this picture are clustered around another vessel to speed the transfer of general cargo.

The tug *Resolute* nudges the *Ferngate* into a Locust Point
pier in 1963.

MARYLAND
HISTORICAL
SOCIETY
PHOTOS

Up, Up and Away . . .

SHIPS can transport almost anything, provided a means is found to get the cargo on and off. These Locust Point scenes show the loading of railroad cars, a workboat and a horse.

Largest crane in the Port of Baltimore is this one operated by the Maryland Port Administration at South Locust Point. It is capable of lifting 350 tons.

MARYLAND PORT ADMINISTRATION

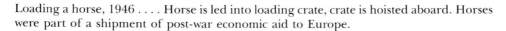

Loading a horse, 1946 . . . . Horse is led into loading crate, crate is hoisted aboard. Horses were part of a shipment of post-war economic aid to Europe.

MARYLAND HISTORICAL SOCIETY

The *Three Brothers* derrick lifts a rail car aboard a ship bound for England in 1946 . . . . Below, the SS *Gadsden* puts locomotives aboard with her own 125-ton booms.

MARYLAND HISTORICAL SOCIETY PHOTOS

Immigrants ready to debark at Locust Point, about 1910.

PEALE MUSEUM

The Immigrants

TOBACCO, cotton and grain exports were the staples of the B & O's 19th century trade, but the most interesting "commodity" was inbound: thousands upon thousands of immigrants, particularly from Germany. In the 1830s and 1840s, Baltimore had especially strong ties with Bremen, whose records showed 57 sailing vessels, with 5,967 passengers, cleared for Baltimore in 1839, compared to 38 ships cleared for New York. Most of these immigrants were landed at Henderson's Wharf in Fells Point. But sailing ships couldn't keep up with the demand for passenger space; after briefly operating a steamship line of its own, the B & O Railroad made arrangements with the North German Lloyd Line to establish a strong steamship passenger service into Baltimore. A huge crowd gathered at the new B & O pier at Locust Point on the morning of March 24, 1868, to see the *Baltimore* steam in from Bremen to inaugu-

rate the service. The guns at Fort McHenry roared out a salute. At that time, Baltimore was almost a German city. A fourth of her 160,000 white inhabitants had been born in Germany and half of the remainder were of German descent.

Not all of the immigrants remained in Baltimore. Many boarded trains inside the pier sheds and immediately headed west. For a time Baltimore ranked second only to Ellis Island in New York in numbers of immigrants handled, with ships arriving from Scandinavia and the British Isles, as well as Germany. A new immigration station (the present Naval Reserve quarters) was built near Fort McHenry in 1916. But World War I brought suspension of the Bremen service. The North German Lloyd Line resumed the service in 1926, but Baltimore never recovered her position as an important passenger port.

B & O RAILROAD MUSEUM

Ships air sails at B & O immigrant pier in this 1880s painting by Herbert Stitt which hangs
in the B & O Railroad Museum . . . . Below, Str. *Baltimore* at the Locust Point pier.

MARYLAND HISTORICAL SOCIETY

This 1865 view by E. Sachse & Co. shows the fort during the Civil War . . . . Confederate prisoners are being led up the road to a prisoner-of-war compound at middle left of the drawing. Other barracks are for federal troops.

Fort McHenry

SHORTLY after midnight on Tuesday, Sept. 13, 1814, after putting an invasion force ashore on North Point the previous day, British naval forces began their famous bombardment of Fort McHenry.

"Baltimore is a doomed town," the British had proclaimed, but events proved otherwise. The rout of the land force is described on page 159. The total failure of the naval operation is attributed to the inability of the British fleet to get close enough—either to support the land forces or inflict serious damage on the fort. The ship channel was tricky at best, and Gen. Sam Smith, a Revolutionary War figure who was in charge of the city's defense, had made things more difficult for the British by blocking the way with sunken ships. Anticipating that some British ships might slip through and attack Fort McHenry from the rear, Gen. Smith set up batteries at Forts Babcock and Covington on the Middle Branch. The thorough preparations payed off when a 1,200-man landing force was repulsed off Fort Covington Tuesday night.

The ineffectual bombardment continued throughout the day Tuesday and into the early

MARYLAND HISTORICAL SOCIETY

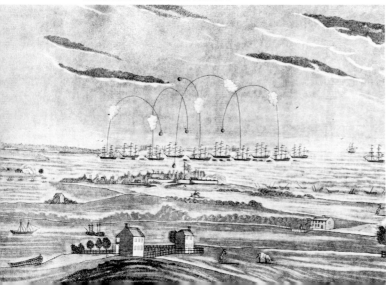

A sketch shows the British attack on Fort McHenry . . . . Established as Fort Whetstone at the time of the American Revolution, it was one of the first forts set up to defend the new republic.

hours Wednesday morning. One of the witnesses was a lawyer from Frederick, Maryland, Francis Scott Key. Key and Col. John S. Skinner sailed out to the British forces under a flag of truce to seek the release of a Maryland physician, Dr. Beanes, who had been captured earlier. Key and Col. Skinner were well received by the British, but were forbidden to return while the bombardment was underway. When dawn came Wednesday, Key was so elated to see the American flag still flying over the fort that he began penning a poem on the back of a letter he had in his pocket. He finished the effort that evening in Baltimore, and the following day his uncle, Judge Joseph H. Nicholson, had it struck off in handbills at the office of the *Baltimore American*. Judge Nicholson also discovered that the verses could be sung to the tune of an English drinking song "Anacreon in Heaven." Key's "Star-Spangled Banner" rapidly became popular but was not officially adopted by Congress as the national anthem until March 4, 1931.

The spot where Key anchored and watched the bombardment is marked by a red, white and blue Coast Guard buoy, just west of Key Bridge near Dundalk Terminal. The flag that inspired Key was made by Mary Pickersgill whose home on East Pratt St. is preserved as "The Flag House."

MARYLAND HISTORICAL SOCIETY

The *Argonaut*

AN EVENT of possibly greater long-range military significance than the bombardment of Fort McHenry took place just outside the fort about 80 years later. This was the construction of Simon Lake's submarine, the *Argonaut*, at the Columbian Iron Works on the site of the present Fort McHenry ship repair yard of Bethlehem Steel. The little vessel, 36 feet long and 9 feet wide, was built on a hand-to-mouth budget in competition with a well-funded Navy Department submarine experiment that failed. It was successfully tested off Fort McHenry in 1897.

Lake's submarine was operated by a 30 horsepower gasoline engine whose exhaust fumes were vented to the surface by a 20-foot pipe. A similar pipe brought in fresh air. In deep water the pipes could be extended by hoses and floats. The sub was propelled along the bottom by two large cog wheels forward and one in the rear. It made successful trips to Norfolk and up the Atlantic Coast, prompting a congratulatory telegram from Jules Verne.

The sub introduced features that have endured to present times: it used ballast water to submerge; it carried a dynamo and storage batteries and could stay under for 10 hours without air; it sported a searchlight and a chamber in the bow where divers could go in and out to a bell to perform salvage work, which was the craft's principal intended purpose. Simon Lake was rightfully recognized as father of the modern submarine. Today submarines are used to conceal nuclear weapons in the ocean depths and are essential elements in U. S. and Soviet military strategy.

U. S. COAST GUARD

Where Key watched the bombardment.

THE 10-story American Sugar Co. (now Amstar) refinery—with the big Domino sign—was opened on Locust Point in 1922. It was the largest and most modern sugar plant in the world, capable of turning out a billion pounds a year. Inside, the refinery is reminiscent of the engine rooms of a great ship, with catwalks among the pipes and conduits, boilers and vats, and a hum of machinery running smoothly around the clock. The essential purpose of the plant is to receive brown raw sugar from the West Indies, Central and South America and transform it into the snow-white crystalline sugar that Americans buy in the grocery store.

The air photo above, taken in 1922, shows a harbor institution next to the sugar plant that is now remembered only by old-timers: the William E. Woodall & Co. shipyard. This yard built and repaired a number of Baltimore's passenger steamers, including the *Emma Giles*. It also looked after the big cargo schooners.

The Woodall yard had the harbor's first dry-dock, a floating affair built at the Reeder wharf on Federal Hill in 1874. The 270 foot by 60-foot dry-dock was a harbor landmark for 62 years. It could be sunk in 30 minutes to pick up a ship in need of paint or repair, and handled 50 or more vessels a year. When the Woodall operation closed in 1929 the drydock was moved to the Patapsco Dry Dock Co. on Locust Point, and in 1934 it was towed down the Bay to the Norfolk Dredging Co. in Norfolk.

The photo shows three Bay steamers in the yard with the one on the right raised up in the drydock. Two large schooners are also in for service.

These views from Woodalls shipyard show the sailing vessel *Tusitala* unloading raw sugar at the Locust Point refinery in 1930, and the steamer *Domino* unloading a year later. The old Fells Point-Locust Point ferry boat *Howard W. Jackson* can barely be seen crossing the harbor behind the *Domino*.

MARYLAND
HISTORICAL
SOCIETY
PHOTOS

A view looking forward on the four-masted schooner *Edward L. Swann*, tied up at the Woodall docks in 1935. The four-master *Katherine May* is at right.

I-95 Tunnel

THE largest project in the history of the National Interstate Highway program got underway in 1981 when a hydraulic dredge began excavating a trench under the Patapsco River between Locust Point and Canton. In 1982 workers began lowering giant steel and concrete tubes into the trench, and by 1985 the connected tubes were open to traffic, carrying eight lanes of Interstate-95 the main roadway between New England and Florida. The tunnel came in under its $825 million budget, with the Federal Government picking up 90 percent of the tab.

The tunnel construction process can be seen in this air view, looking east over Fort McHenry. In the immediate foreground, four temporary access tubes poke up out of the water from sections already laid. Further out, the catamaran "lay barge" prepares to lower another section as a tug and barge arrive with concrete to strengthen it and weight it down. Next comes the "screed barge" which spreads and levels a two-foot gravel bed on which the sections rest. Across the river, the dredge can be seen excavating the trench just south of the Lehigh cement towers on old Lazaretto Point in Canton. A string of pipe leads off from the dredge, carrying the spoil to the Sea Girt disposal site barely visible at top of picture.

Launching a tunnel . . . . Tunnel sections were built by the Wiley Manufacturing Co. in Port Deposit on the Susquehanna River and towed 12 hours down Chesapeake Bay to the tunnel site. Thirty-two of these sections are needed for the more than mile-long portion of the tunnel that lies under water between the ventilation buildings. Each section is 340 feet long, 82 feet wide and 42 feet high. Those in the freighter channel must be buried sufficiently to allow 50 feet of clearance for passage of ships overhead. The sections are laid side by side in two rows to provide eight lanes of traffic.

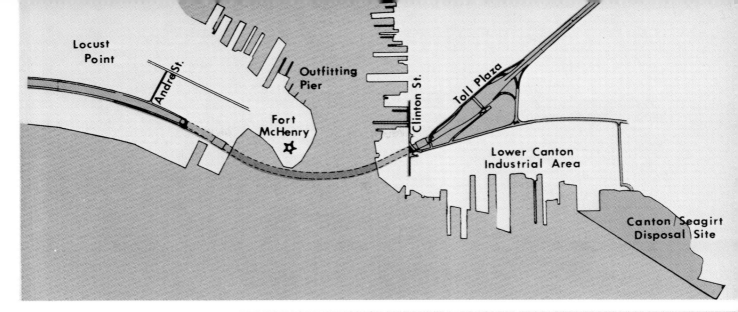

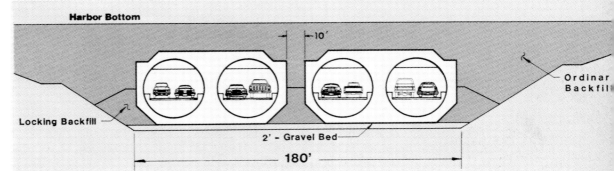

PHOTOS COURTESY
CITY OF BALTIMORE,
RICK LIPPENHOLZ

Cross section of the eight-lane tunnel.

Canton Sea Girt disposal site, looking east, with the former Western Electric plant on left, Dundalk Terminal and Key Bridge at top of photo . . . When the spoil settled, the site became a major container terminal with three 1000-foot-long berths.

Federal Hill from World Trade Center.

Federal Hill was not always the manicured park one sees today . . . It was a rough cliff of red clay and sand when Capt. John Smith found it, and was still so when H. H. Clark made this daguerreotype about 1851, looking south from approximately the present site of Harborplace.

PEALE MUSEUM

EILEEN P. KELLY

Chapter 9

Federal Hill

WHEN the first European explorer, Capt. John Smith, sailed up the Patapsco River in 1608, he took note of the large hill which bounds the present Inner Harbor to the south. The hill's red clay reminded him of a substance known in Europe as bole Armoniac, used in cosmetics, and because of this he named the river Bolus. Historians agree that Smith's Bolus and the Indians' Patapsco were the same river. For a long time the promentory was known as John Smith's hill, but on Dec. 22, 1788, Baltimoreans staged a great parade through the city, culminating in food and fireworks on the hill, all in honor of the Maryland General Assembly's ratification of the Federal Constitution. The hill and surrounding neighborhood has carried the name Federal Hill since that day. This view shows, on the far right, the Maryland Science Center, built on the site where Thomas Morgan opened the hill's first shipyard in 1773, and on the far left, Bethlehem Steel's Key Highway ship repair yards, where work was performed on everything from tugboats to supertankers more than 1,000 feet in length.

MARYLAND HISTORICAL SOCIETY

By the time of the American Revolution, small shipyards were springing up at the base of Federal Hill, followed by engine shops, breweries, small iron and steel mills, fertilizer and chemical plants, ice storage houses, canneries, glass factories and other enterprises . . . . The above view, looking east from the hill about 1870, was part of a series sold for enjoyment on the home "stero" (stereoscope)—a hand-held device that gave a three dimensional effect when the cards were viewed through the binocular-like eyepiece.

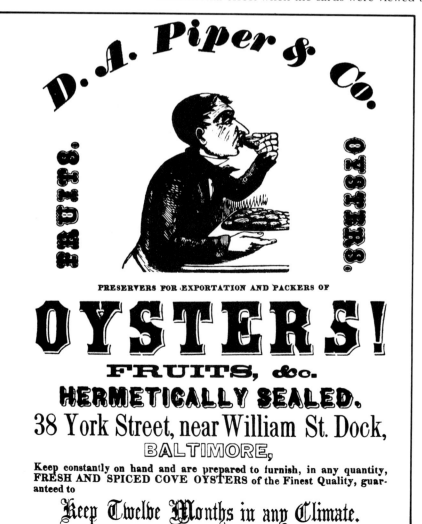

Chas Reeder

Steamboats and Engines

BALTIMORE'S first steamboat, the *Chesapeake*, was built at McElderry's Wharf, on the north side of the harbor. The engine was fabricated and installed by Charles Reeder, who came down from Pennsylvania and established a shop on Federal Hill. The 130-foot paddlewheel steamer was put on the run to Frenchtown, at the head of the Bay, from which her passengers could be taken overland to Philadelphia:

> The appliances for her navigation were simple and crude. A pilot stood at the bow who called out a course to a man amidships, and he to the helmsman. There were no bells to signal the engine, but the captain conveyed his commands by word of mouth or by stamping his heels on the woodwork over the engine. The boat had been running six months when the engineer ac-

Model of the *Chesapeake*, Baltimore's first steamboat, at Maryland Historical Society.

cidentally discovered that he could reverse the engine and back her.*

Federal Hill became the center for steamboat construction. Charles Reeder's company built engines for 80 vessels, including five built keel up by the company itself. A Reeder launching was marked by a touch of class. The *Susquehanna* was christened in 1898 with a flask of water from the river of her name. The *Queen Anne* was christened the following year by release of four doves from a cage in her bow, Japanese style.

Another pioneer engine builder at Federal Hill, John Watchman, was less fortunate than Charles Reeder. His engine in the Baltimore Steam Packet Company's *Medora* exploded on the ship's trial run April 14, 1842, and 26 persons died, including the passenger line's first president, Andrew F. Henderson. *Medora* was rebuilt, given a Reeder boiler, and rechristened *Herald*. She remained in service 43 years, lastly as a tug on the Hudson River.

* Johnston's History of Cecil County.

Explosion of the *Medora*.

Porter's observation tower can be seen in this view of Federal Hill during the Civil War . . . . MARYLAND HISTORICAL SOCIETY The sympathies of Baltimore were divided during this conflict, and to insure control, Federal forces occupied the hill in May, 1861, building barracks and external fortifications and aiming cannons at the heart of the city.

Observation Tower

FOR more than a century, from 1797 until 1902, Federal Hill was topped by a tall observation tower, used to signal the appearance of ships heading up the Bay to Baltimore harbor.

Capt. David Porter obtained 300 subscriptions from local businessmen to construct the first wooden tower, which was augmented by lookout stations at North Point and Bodkin Point. The ships carried flags of their owners, and when these flags were spotted by powerful telescopes, an identical flag was flown from Porter's observatory, where it could be seen by all the merchants and chandlers in the harbor. This advance notice of ship arrivals meant important savings of time and money to shippers and suppliers.

In 1888, nine years after Federal Hill was designated as a public park, the Park Commission built a new tower, with an ice cream stand at its base, to replace Porter's sturdy observatory. The ungainly Victorian ediface rocked in high winds, and a summer squall of 1902 knocked it over. It was not replaced. Telephone and telegraph, and more recently, radio, supplanted the signal flags in giving advance word of ship arrivals. Today the information is supplied through the Baltimore Maritime Exchange, located at the Recreation Pier, Fells Point, and a record of ship arrivals and departures is carried each day in the Baltimore papers.

The ill-fated second tower.

MARYLAND HISTORICAL SOCIETY

Threats to the Hill

FEDERAL Hill has survived three man-inspired threats to its very existence.

In 1838, Dr. Thomas H. Buckler proposed to level the hill and use the sand and clay to fill the inner harbor basin. This plan, he maintained, would rid the city of the pestilential water of the shallow basin, admit fresh air from the river, and greatly facilitate transportation within the city.

In 1962, the Maryland Port Authority proposed construction of a superhighway through Federal Hill, with a low bridge across the neck of the Inner Harbor to the docks of East Baltimore. The plan would have destroyed the historic districts of Federal Hill and Fells Point and turned the Inner Harbor into a downtown lagoon, inaccessible to tall ships.

It is a tribute to the feistyness of Baltimore property owners that these schemes were ultimately defeated, despite powerful backing.

The third threat was perhaps more insidious. During the 1800s private interests began burrowing into the hill to obtain sand for glass-making and building purposes, and clay for pipes and pottery. As a consequence, the hill is riddled with deep unmapped tunnels, some of which occasionally are exposed. Brewers used the tunnels to store kegs of beer and whiskey. Federal troops stored ammunition and supplies in them during the Civil War. Interesting details about the tunnels can be found in Norman G. Rukert's book, *Federal Hill.*

Inner Harbor bridge proposed in 1962.

The Thin Ship

HALF the town turned out, including hundreds aboard the S.S. *Columbia,* to watch the launching of the *Howard Cassard* at Federal Hill on Nov. 6, 1890. The *Cassard* was perhaps the most improbable vessel ever put together by grown men. From the side it looked reasonable enough: 222 feet long, 18 feet from deck to keel, and portholes to light every stateroom. But look at the view head-on: The vessel was only 16 feet wide! It looked like one of those skinny fishes in an aquarium. Robert M. Freyer, who designed the ship, was not a naval architect, and neither was Howard Cassard, a Baltimore lard mogul who agreed to back him. The idea was that with virtually no bow wave to push aside, the vessel could cross the Atlantic in a few days. The narrow cabins were set up like Pullman berths, with an aisle between. A 34-ton iron keel was provided for stability.

The people in this photo did not see the *Cassard* launched that day. It stuck on the ways. But Freyer tried again the following day, and, with the tug *Britannia* pulling, managed to get his strange ship afloat. The flaw in the *Cassard*'s design showed itself instantly: unlike the aquarium fishes, the *Howard Cassard* had no means of holding itself on an even keel. The vessel leaned on its side and its mast struck and carried away the smokestack of another assisting tug, the *Baltimore.* Undaunted, Freyer had the ship taken to Woodall's shipyard for repairs, after which he invited guests for a trial run. This too, ended in failure. The *Cassard* again listed alarmingly, the guests panicked, and her only voyage was cut short after a mile. She returned to dock where she remained for 12 years until sold for scrap.

The Shipyards

FOR many years, the largest Federal Hill shipyard was the Skinner yard at the foot of Cross Street. Barks and brigantines were built here for the coffee trade and, between 1860 and 1890, the yard turned out nine Chesapeake Bay steam packets. Just to the north were the Booz Brothers yard, which moved to the hill from Canton in 1879, and Redman and Vane, which was founded in 1917 and specialized in repair of wooden sailing ships.

The present Key Highway was cut through the area in 1913. A year later the Skinner yard went into receivership. It was renamed Baltimore Dry Dock & Shipbuilding Co., and was acquired by Bethlehem Shipbuilding Corp. in 1921. The Booz and Redman and Vane yards were absorbed by Bethlehem immediately after the outbreak of World War II, when Bethlehem needed more space to fulfill war contracts. Bethlehem's Key Highway repair yard handled more than 2,600 ships during the war years, installing armorplate and gun platforms on merchant ships, converting passenger ships to troop transports, and repairing ships that were damaged. The yard closed in 1983.

PHOTOS FROM MARYLAND HISTORICAL SOCIETY

A tugboat in drydock for repairs. early 1900s.

The sidewheeler *Federal Hill* (ex. *Avalon*) at Booz Brothers yard, July 1939. A year later she was cut down to a barge.

THE HUGHES CO.—MARYLAND HISTORICAL SOCIETY COLLECTION

Bethlehem's Key Highway ship repair yard in the late 1930s .... This sweeping view takes in Fells Point, Canton and Locust Point. A large warehouse dominates Fells Point behind the ships at left, preceding the Allied Chemical chrome plant which occupied the site from 1950 to 1985. Photo at left shows this same panorama around the turn of the century.

Chapter 10

Inner Harbor

AFTER passing the general cargo piers of Locust Point, a traveler to Baltimore's Inner Harbor can almost navigate by smell. First, to port, comes the unmistakable scent of Ivory and other famous soaps being made at the Proctor & Gamble plant, opened in 1930. Then comes the pleasant smell of raw sugar, being unloaded almost any time of day or night at the Amstar (Domino) sugar plant. Beyond the sugar refinery, one steers northwest, between ghost sounds and oders of the old Bethlehem Key Highway ship repair yards, to the left, and the Allied Chemical chrome plant, to the right, into the aromatic embrace of the McCormick spice plant at the head of the Inner Harbor.

The Inner Harbor is Baltimore's enchantress, the magical shoreline that has won national attention. The present-day development is traced to 1963, when Abel Wolman, a prominent local water resources engineer, returned from a visit to Europe with glowing tales of Stockholm's harbor. Wolman urged Mayor Theodore R. McKeldin to develop a similar plan for Baltimore, enlisting Philadelphia

PHOTO: DAVID W. HARP, SUNPAPERS

designer David A. Wallace, who had planned the city's Charles Center renewal project in 1959. Wallace credits his partner, Thomas A. Todd, for the resultant masterplan, which drew this comment from *Progressive Architecture* magazine in April 1965:

Inner Harbor . . . emerges as a candidate for the best use of water and open land in post-war U. S. urban renewal. Instead of cutting the water off from the city, as almost all our cities do, Baltimore—if this plan is followed—will thrust the living, 24-hours-a-day city into intimate and vivacious contact with the harbor whence it sprang.

The harbor has developed largely in keeping with Todd's plan. The photographs and descriptions on the following pages provide a clockwise tour of public attractions. Locations can be seen on the map. With the exception of the Industrial Museum, all points of interest are accessible from one another by foot; however, for the footsore. a refreshing respite can be found in the water taxis that circle the harbor in either direction.

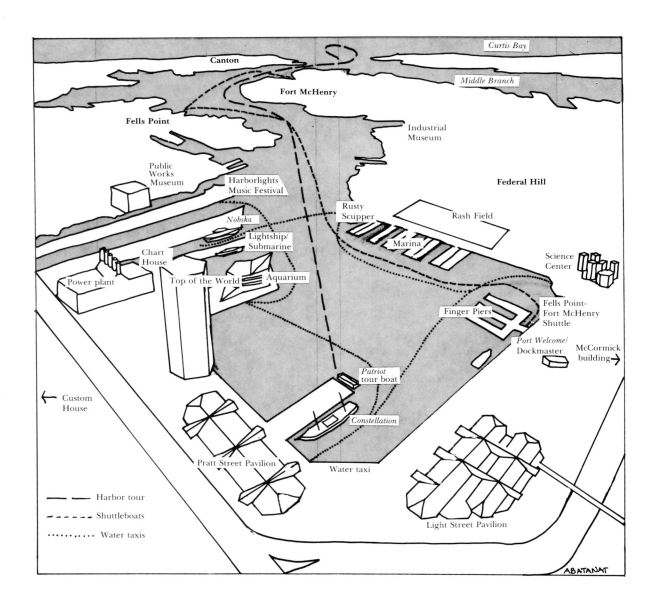

Baltimore Museum of Industry, 1415 Key Highway. This was organized on a shoestring in 1981. Demonstrations include a belt-driven machine shop, a loft garment shop, a working print shop and a representation of the Port. Behind the museum is the S.S. *Baltimore*, a turn-of-the-century steam tugboat undergoing restoration after spending several years under water on the other side of Chesapeake Bay. The *Baltimore* was once used by the Maryland Port Administration for public tours of the harbor and the museum hopes to return it to similar use eventually. Phone 727-4808.

Rusty Scupper/Inner Harbor Marina, Key Highway. This glass and wood-beam structure, opened in 1982, does double duty as home for a restaurant and marina. The Rusty Scupper Restaurant offers spendid views of the harbor from every table, and the marina offers 158 boat slips, including water, electricity and showers. Eighty of the slips are devoted to daily rentals by transient boaters. Reservations are taken and Saturday nights may be booked up months in advance. Phones: Rusty Scupper, 727-3678; Inner Harbor Marina, 837-5339.

Maryland Science Center, Light St. and Key Highway. This $7.2 million brick structure was built by the Maryland Academy of Sciences in 1976 as one of the first public attractions in the harbor. A decade later the fortress-like exterior was given a facelift and a spectacular "Imax" big screen theater was added to keep in step with the harbor's tourist boom. Exhibits include slide shows, a hands-on "science arcade" and live demonstrations of scientific phenomena. The Davis Planetarium offers daily shows on astronomy. Exhibits feature the city, geology, Chesapeake Bay, computers and energy. Open some evenings. Phone 685-5225.

Fort McHenry-Fells Point Shuttle, Finger Piers opposite McCormick Bldg. Departing every 30 minutes, these boats take visitors "around the bend" to two of Baltimore's most historic places. The ride is about 20 minutes to Fort McHenry, with a stop at Fells Point on the return trip; operates daily Memorial Day through Labor Day. Phone 752-1515.

Bay Lady/Lady Baltimore, 301 Light St. The new 600 passenger "showboat" *Bay Lady* joined Baltimore's harbor fleet in 1988, specializing in luncheon and dinner cruises. She is operated by Harbor Cruises Ltd., in tandem with the 136-foot *Lady Baltimore* which operates day excursions in the tradition of the old Baltimore sidewheelers. *Lady Baltimore*'s cruise schedule features daytrips to Annapolis, St. Michaels or the C&D Canal. Phone 727-3113.

Minnie V, Harborplace Ceremonial Steps. This city-owned Chesapeake Bay skipjack offers narrated tours of the old harbor under sail, with capacity of 24 passengers. Managed by the Maryland Historical Society, the classic vessel dredges for oysters in the winter, returning to the harbor in the spring. The summer program is operated by Ocean World Institute, Inc., 522-4214. Another sailing vessel, the 149-passenger **Clipper City**, began operations in the harbor in fall of 1985, offering charters and three-hour public cruises (phone 539-6063).

Seawall and Finger Piers. Dockage at the finger piers and alongside the lively seawall promenade is open to boaters on a first-come, first-served basis, with a minimum $2 fee for the first four hours (as of 1988), and no reservations accepted. In theory, boaters can pull in and walk to Harborplace for a snack or meal but space is at a premium on summer weekends and it may be necessary to anchor in the mucky bottom between Constellation Pier and the Aquarium, or head for the rougher piers east of the lightship. The dockmaster keeps office just off the finger piers. Power and water hookups are available. Phone 396-3174.

Harborplace, 301 Light St. Some 135 shops, restaurants and food stalls of every shape, size and ethnic origin are packed into two glass and metal pavilions that now rank among the world's liveliest retail operations in sales per square foot.

In December 1978 the City of Baltimore struck a deal with developer James W. Rouse by the terms of which the Rouse Co. built the Pratt Street shopping pavilion and Light Street food pavilion on 3.2 acres of city-owned land. The pavilions opened to great fanfare on July 2, 1980, though their conception was not without controversy. Some Baltimoreans felt they would intrude on the tranquility of the harbor promenade. Mayor William Donald Schaefer successfully engineered a referendum to assure construction of the buildings. The objections have largely been forgotton as hordes jam the popular pavilions.

Under the 1978 agreement, Rouse Co. pays the city an annual basic rent of $100,000, plus 25 percent of cash remaining after deducting a 10 percent operating profit, 10 percent on equity investment and other expenses. Individual entrepreneurs reportedly pay, depending on location, anywhere from $48 to $96 a square foot annual rent, plus utilities, to operate in this prime commercial space.

U.S. Frigate *Constellation*, Constellation Dock, Pratt St. The 176-foot U.S.F. *Constellation* was built in Baltimore by David Stodder in 1797 and returned to the city as a museum in 1955 after a storybook naval career.

She is said to be the oldest ship in the world continuously afloat. She defeated the French ships *L'Insurgente* and *La Vengeance* in her first five years of service, engaged pirates off the Barbary Coast in 1802, fought the British in the War of 1812, opened U.S. trade with China in the 1840s, helped break up the slave trade off Africa in the early 1860s, transported food to Ireland during the famine of 1880, served as a training ship at Annapolis, and was commissioned by President Roosevelt as flagship of the Atlantic Fleet, moored at Newport, Rhode Island, in World War II.

From 1853 to 1855 the *Constellation* was in the Portsmouth, Virginia, Navy shipyard. This was a period when the Navy had money for repairs but none for new construction. The ship that emerged was 12 feet longer and was said to contain 34 percent of the original timbers. A controversy arose among maritime buffs as to whether the refurbished ship was really the *Constellation* or a new ship with the same name. The argument was akin to John Locke's philosophical question: If you patch a pair of socks until there is nothing but patches, is it still the same pair of socks?

Visitors can tour the ship from spar deck to orlop. Open daily to 4 p.m., later in summer. Phone 539-1797.

Baltimore *Patriot* Harbor Tours, Constellation Pier. From mid-April through October the *Patriot* boats carry visitors on a 1½ hour narrated tour of Baltimore harbor, past Fort McHenry to Fort Carroll and the Key Bridge and back. Tour boat passengers will see ships from all over the world at the piers and berths of Locust Point, Canton and Dundalk. The boats depart hourly in peak season, three times daily in spring and fall. Phone 685-4288.

Paddleboats, next to Constellation Pier. Visitors can satisfy the urge to get out on the water through a rental fleet of 69 paddleboats maintained by Harbor Boating, Inc. Open April-October, with paddling possible up to 11 p.m. on summer nights. The company also operates the "water taxi" service which connects the various piers. Phone 547-0090. For those without leg muscles, Trident Electric Boats Ltd. operates a fleet of 26 battery-powered boats from a dock just east of the Trade Center. Phone 539-1837.

World Trade Center/Top of the World, 401 E. Pratt St. For a stunning perspective on where you are going in Baltimore, or where you have been, no public place matches the observation floor of the World Trade Center, which features exhibits, a gift shop and giant windows on five sides. The $22 million Trade Center was designed by I. M. Pei and opened in 1977. It is home for the Maryland Port Administration and many of the ship lines and agencies. Sale of tickets to the observation floor ends at 4:30 p.m. (9:30 p.m. on summer Fridays and Saturdays). Phone 837-4515.

National Aquarium in Baltimore, Pier 3, Pratt St. The crown jewel of the Inner Harbor, the $21.3 million National Aquarium, has had a waiting line snaking to its dramatic tetrahedral entrance almost every day since it opened in August 1981. Marine biologists and engineers control the environment of over one million gallons of water to care for and display some 5,000 creatures in natural-looking settings. Highlights include an outdoor seal pool, a whale tank, a 335,000 gallon Atlantic coral reef (largest in the U.S.), a 220,000 gallon shark tank, a tropical rain forest, and displays showing the range of aquatic life from mountain stream to seashore. Ramps, bridges and escalators carry visitors over, around and through the gigantic glass-walled tanks and displays while recorded fish sounds and gurgles play overhead. In 1987 work commenced on an addition consisting of a Marine Mammal Pavilion and additional classrooms on neighboring Pier 4. Open daily to 5 p.m., 8 p.m. Friday through Sunday. Phone 576-3810 (but expect a recorded man sound).

Custom House Call Room, 103 S. Gay St. An unadvertised maritime and architectural attraction is the Call Room of the U.S. Custom House at Lombard and Gay streets, a block north of the Aquarium. The classic granite structure was started in 1903, on the site of an earlier custom house, at a time when captains from arriving vessels were still carrying their manifests and clearing papers to the Custom House before their ships could be unloaded.

The giant Call Room, where the captains brought their papers, is 50 by 95 feet, with a 35-foot-high ceiling decorated by a huge canvas showing 10 sailing ships entering Baltimore harbor on a summer morning. There are 28 smaller paintings and five lunettes. All are by marine artist Francis D. Millet, who went down with the *Titanic* in 1912. The room and its paintings were restored for the 1976 Bicentennial, but few uses have been found for it. The public may view it during working hours.

Harrison's at Pier 5. This $20 million inn and restaurant complex, opened in 1989, is one of the first elements of a Maritime Center expected to gradually replace the parking lots of Piers 5 and 6 at the eastern end of the Inner Harbor. The 76-room inn and home style Chesapeake Bay restaurant is operated by the Harrison Organization of Tilghman Island. The vintage Seven Foot Knoll lighthouse was moved from the mouth of the Patapsco River to mark the tip of the pier south of the restaurant.

Baltimore Maritime Museum, relocating to Pier 5 in 1992. Here one can walk through a submarine, a lightship and 327-foot Coast Guard cutter, all of historical significance. The 311-foot submarine *Torsk*, built in 1944, fired the last torpedo and sank the last Japanese combatant ships of World War II. Later, as a training ship, it set an all-time world record of 11,884 dives. The 133-foot lightship *Chesapeake*, really a floating lighthouse, served for 29 years to mark the entrance to Chesapeake Bay off the Virginia Capes. The cutter *Taney* is the last vessel afloat to survive the 1941 attack on Pearl Harbor. It was decommissioned in 1986 after 50 years of service. Pier closes at 4:30 p.m., 8 p.m. during the summer. Phone 396-3854.

Power Plant, Pier 4. A dominant structure in the Inner Harbor is the old three-section brick steam and electric power plant of Baltimore Gas & Electric Co. The city acquired the idle plant for $1,650,000 in 1977 and began looking for a good use. In 1985, Six Flags Corp. opened it as a family entertainment center, but the project failed and a new use was sought. Directly south is the Chart House Restaurant, created out of an outbuilding of the power plant. Ship models and sailing photos are part of the dramatic motif.

Harborlights Music Festival, Pier 6, Pratt St. This imaginative tentlike outdoor concert pavilion is a popular attraction on summer evenings. It opened in 1981 with such varied quality fare as Ella Fitzgerald, Yehudi Menuhin, Robert Merrill and the Preservation Hall Jazz Band. Seats range from $12.50 to $3 to nothing at all for those who come by boat or sit on the seawall across Jones Falls. Phone 679-2399.

Public Works Museum/Sewage Pumping Station, President Street at Eastern Avenue. A Public Works Museum was opened in 1982 at the ornate brick and copper Sewage Pumping Station. The museum features a $500,000 "streetscape" demonstrating the below-ground marvels at a typical street intersection.

The Sewage Pumping Station, built in 1911, is a marvel in itself. Until that time, Baltimore had one of the worst sewage systems of any American city. Cesspools abounded; what piped sewage there was drained directly into the harbor, including vegetable refuse from shoreside canneries. The noxious odors were brought well up into the heart of the city. "You could smell the harbor for miles and new paint on vessels coming into the harbor was oxidized," one observer recalled.

To set the situation right, the city built what for that time was the largest "trickling filter" sewage treatment facility in the world, at a site on Back River, east of the city. At the same time, throughout the city, sewage outlets were diverted from the storm drains and connected to lines leading to Back River, culminating in a five and one-half mile long gravity drain 11 feet high and 12 feet wide.

Because a third of the city was on ground too low to drain to Back River by gravity, the pipes for this part of the city were led to the pumping station. Here, three steam-driven pumps, again the largest of their kind in the world, were installed to force the sewage up a 60-foot rise to Bond and Fayette streets, a mile to the northeast, where it feeds into the tunnel to Back River.

The pumping station includes a screen room, to protect the pumps from debris, a boiler room and coal bin, no longer used because of conversion to diesel-run pumps, and an emergency bypass into the harbor which, fortunately, has never been used.

In time, the Back River plant has become inadequate to the needs of a growing metropolis. Disputes have arisen over the discharging of water into Back River and the disposal of sludge on nearby farms. An engineering report suggested in 1928 that the material gives best results when used to fertilize white potatoes, cabbage and corn.

Beal-Ti-Mor

BALTIMORE derives its name from a town on the eastern shore of St. George's Channel, County Cork, in Ireland. The original Irish Beal-Ti-Mor means great place or circle of Baal, the Sun-God, erected on that site in pagan times.

George Calvert, a Yorkshireman, was created Baron of Baltimore (Lord Baltimore) by James I of England in 1625. His son Cecilius, second Lord Baltimore, was made Lord Proprietary of England's first Province, Maryland, in 1632. The following year, Cecilius sent his brother, Leonard, to take possession of the province as Lieutenant-General and Governor. The colonizers came on the *Ark* and the *Dove* in the spring of 1634 and settled near the mouth of the Potomac. Baltimore County, with boundaries far more extensive than today, was established in 1659. The town of Baltimore in Ireland, once a leading trading port of the Phoenicians, has dwindled to a small village, while its American namesake has become one of the great seaports of the world.

In 1668, more than a half century after the visit of Capt. John Smith, and 34 years after the arrival of the first settlers in southern Maryland, Thomas Cole obtained a warrant for 550 acres of land in Baltimore County, at the place where Jones Falls enters the Patapsco River—the present Inner Harbor. He called the surrounding basin of water Cole's Harbor. It was a shallow basin in those days and saw few ships. The Jones Falls outlet was a wide marsh. Water extended north to the present Water and Gay streets and west to the present Charles Street. One dirt road, later to be called Calvert Street, led to the water, and here a county tobacco wharf was built, about where Lombard crosses Calvert today.

In 1729, some local entrepreneurs obtained a charter to establish Baltimore Town on a portion of Cole's land. A few years later another charter was obtained for a town to the east, on the other side of Jones Falls, to be called Jones Town (now Old Town) after David Jones who had settled and opened a store there in 1661.

Among those involved in the Jones Town development were the Fell brothers, Edward and William. Edward had arrived from England in 1726 and set up a store on what was to be the Jones Town site. William, a carpenter from Lancashire, arrived four years later and purchased a 100-acre tract a mile or so to the south, on an indentation of water called Copus Harbor, where he erected a mansion and small shipyard. By the time of his death in 1746, William Fell had expanded his Copus Harbor holdings to 1,100 acres. His son Edward laid these off as the town of Fells Point in 1763.

No one could have foreseen at that time, more than 200 years ago, that these tiny hamlets, Baltimore Town, Jones Town and Fells Point, would one day form the core of a great American city.

Laying out Baltimore town.

R. MCGILL MACKALL—MARYLAND HISTORICAL SOCIETY COLLECTION

HISTORY OF BALTIMORE CITY AND COUNTY

Baltimore Inner Harbor, 1752 . . . . This is how the town looked—with 25 houses, 200 residents and one pier in shallow water—when Dr. John Stevenson shipped an experimental cargo of flour to Ireland. The trade he initiated helped turn the sleepy harbor into a major seaport. This view from Federal Hill is based on a drawing by John Moale, whose father owned land and operated a store on the Middle Branch of the Patapsco, a few miles to the south.

MARYLAND HISTORICAL SOCIETY

The first piers . . . . Cole's harbor was very shallow at the county wharf, so local merchants began the construction of long finger piers in an effort to reach navigable water. The first such piers are shown in this 1780 map. William Buchanan and John Smith built long wharves of pine cord in 1759. William Spears built a 1,000-foot pier five years later. In 1783, after this map was drawn, the Ellicott brothers built a wharf at Pratt and Light streets to export flour produced at their giant mill west of the city.

MARYLAND HISTORICAL SOCIETY

Baltimore after the American Revolution . . . . This map was drawn in 1792, four years before Baltimore was incorporated as a city. By this time, Jones Town (upper center) and Fells Point (lower right) had been brought within the Town's boundaries and the population was growing rapidly. At North Point, which commands a view of the entrance to the river, an observer in 1796 kept track of vessel traffic with a telescope. He counted 109 ships, 162 brigs, 350 schooners and sloops, and 5,464 assorted Chesapeake Bay craft all making their way toward Baltimore harbor, indicating the extent to which Baltimore now dominated Bay commerce.

102

MARYLAND HISTORICAL SOCIETY

Buildup of the piers . . . . In the 1860s, the Baltimore lithography firm E. Sachse & Co. sent teams of artists out to record every building in the city. The project took several years. The result was a series of "birds-eye" views, on panels large enough to fill a wall. This section of a view published in 1869 shows the dramatic change at the mouth of Jones Falls. Compare it with the map on the preceding page, made some 75 years earlier, when the entire area south of Eastern Avenue and west of Bond Street was under water.

PEALE MUSEUM

A daguerreotype by H. H. Clark showing the harbor about 1851 . . . The new steamer *Bertha Harassowitz* is in the foreground.

The harbor as it looked about 1872.

MARYLAND HISTORICAL SOCIETY

The Steamboat Era

THE Inner Harbor always lagged behind Fells Point as a mooring site for deep-draft ocean vessels, but it was ideally suited to the shallow-draft paddlewheel steamboats that began to ply the Chesapeake Bay in the early 1800s. For more than a century, until trucks, highways and the distractions of war brought their eclipse at the start of World War II, the steamboats dominated the Inner Harbor.

Baltimore's steamboat expert, H. Graham Wood, classifies the boats that carried passengers and freight from the Light and Pratt Street piers into four general categories.

The Baltimore-Philadelphia steamboats were the first in operation, beginning in 1813—a year when the young American nation, and Baltimore in particular, was still at war with the British. The first

Philadelphia boats ran up the Bay to Frenchtown, and their passengers were then taken overland by stagecoach to the Delaware River for an additional water journey. Later a rail line was built from Philadelphia to the head of the Bay to pick up boat passengers. In 1829, a narrow canal was cut through from the Bay to the Delaware River, enabling the thin ships of the Ericksson Line (so named for the type of propeller they used) to provide overnight through service.

The second category of steamboat service, between Baltimore and Norfolk, began in 1817. For many years this service was monopolized by the Baltimore Steam Packet Co., but at the time of the Civil War a New York-based company came in, advertising itself as the "new" Bay line. The Baltimore Steam Packet Co. countered by reminding

Light Street about 1885.

PEALE MUSEUM

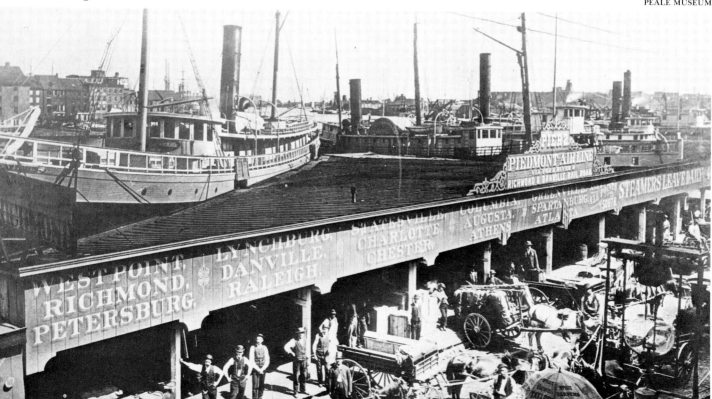

patrons it was the "Old Bay Line," a nickname that was to last for a hundred years.

The Old Bay Line was presented with more durable competition when the Chesapeake Steamship Co. began service to Hampton Roads in 1896. The competition lasted until 1941, when the U. S. Government took over boats of both lines for the war effort. The Old Bay Line then bought out its rival and continued the Bay service for another two decades with two boats the government left behind, the *City of Norfolk* and *City of Richmond*, both already 30 years old at the time.

The Norfolk boats were large and swift, traveling 17–18 miles an hour on the 185-mile overnight run. A third category of steamboat had members which were slower and smaller but which followed schedules infinitely more interesting and romantic. These were the river steamers, which left Baltimore with goods and passengers for all parts of the Bay, and might not return to Light Street for two or three days or even a week. Mr. Wood counts 100 old steamboat landings on the eastern shore of the Chesapeake and 150 on the western shore. Baltimore was the outside world to the waterfront communities served by these landings, their source for fertilizer, farm machinery and supplies. In return, they shipped strawberries, potatoes, tobacco, grain, livestock and seafood back to Baltimore for sale. In those days, the Bay steamers and smaller sailing craft were the only practical means of transportation.

A fourth category of Baltimore steamer was the excursion boat. Day-long outings to Tolchester Beach, Betterton Beach, Chesapeake Beach and other resorts were enjoyed by hundreds of thousands. Across the Bay, the ferry docks at Love Point received passengers for the rail trip to Rehoboth on the Atlantic Ocean, while further south the Claiborne docks were the railhead for service to Ocean City. In 1923 the Rehoboth service was dropped and Love Point was made the terminus of the Ocean City line, with a steamer nicknamed "Smoky Joe" providing the waterborne leg from a Light Street pier.

The peak of steamboat operations on the Bay came around 1910. The Pennsylvania Railroad alone, through operating companies, owned 31 Bay steamers. The Pennsylvania abandoned all its river lines in 1932, dismissing captains and crew without pension. Other lines followed suit, one by one. The rail service from Love Point ended in 1947, as more and more people went to the ocean by car. The bridge across the Chesapeake Bay was opened in 1952, so that even the automobile ferries became obsolete. The Old Bay Line finally ended its Norfolk run in 1962.

MARYLAND HISTORICAL SOCIETY

The walking beam . . . . This apparatus was a distinctive feature of the early sidewheelers. Their great steam pistons were set upright, and the walking beam was used to transfer the reciprocating (up and down) thrust of the pistons to the rotary motion of the paddlewheel crankshaft. In later vessels the pistons were laid on their side so that their power could be applied to the crankshaft directly. For excitement and drama, there was nothing in the world that could quite match the sound, smell and sight of the engine room of a paddlewheel steamer.

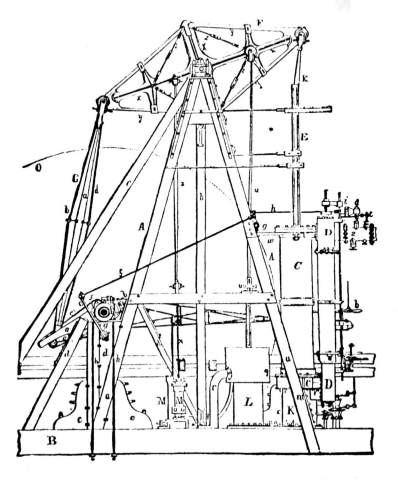

JOHN SHOWERS

Love Point ferry *Philadelphia*, known as Smoky Joe, reverses engines to brake as she approaches her Light Street pier, about 1944 . . . . She made three trips a day, covering the 24-mile run across the Bay in two hours and 20 minutes. Round trip fare was 79 cents. A small restaurant on the upper deck served fresh seafood from Kent Island and pie from a Baltimore bakery.

Oops! . . . . Maryland Gov. Harry W. Nice was thrown to the deck with other state and city officials when the *Golden Harvest* plunged its bow into the *State of Virginia* on July 14, 1936. The accident occurred off Sevenfoot Knoll, at the entrance to the Patapsco, with 263 persons aboard. No one was hurt seriously.

SUNPAPERS

MARYLAND HISTORICAL SOCIETY

Baltimore-Norfolk steamer *City of Richmond* leaves her Pratt Street pier for the last time, Aug. 13, 1964 . . . . She was being towed away to serve as a restaurant at St. Thomas in the Virgin Islands. Unfortunately the journey was delayed in Norfolk into the hurricane season. A big storm hit as she was being towed off the Outer Banks and sent her to the bottom, seven weeks after this photo was taken.

THE flavor of the steamboat days is captured in the following passage written about a voyage in 1926. The little steamboat *Northumberland* has cast off her lines for a voyage down Chesapeake Bay to various landings along the Potomac River. Her ultimate destination is Washington, D.C., about 180 miles by water, 50 minutes by express train. Along the way she will drop off automobile tires, groceries, paint, cement, sugar—whatever supplies are needed by the communities she visits:

As the boat travels along the passengers begin making guesses as to her chances of winning a race that started when she left her pier, at which time three other ships got the same notion. If you have ever been in Baltimore's inner harbor, you will recall the congestion there, with fussy little steamers coming in from and starting out for various points on the Chesapeake and its rivers and creeks.

The *Talbot* has made good headway and the others string along behind. The *Eastern Shore* is second, but the *Northumberland* passes her. Puffing along in the rear is the *Potomac*. But she gains foot by foot and eventually is abreast of us, within speaking distance. For a few minutes it is a bow-and-bow race, the Negro crew calling taunts to each other across the intervening stretch of water.

Slowly the *Potomac* pulls ahead and from her crew come bursts of triumphant laughter and yells of delight, mixed with expressions of amused contempt. Finally, one of the fellows produces a rope and shakes it in the direction of our crew. This is the crowning reproach. For every sailor knows that to "shake a rope at 'em" is the last word in insult—meaning, of course, that a ship at which a rope is shaken is in sore need of being taken in tow.

Fourteen miles from the city the river loses itself in the bay. And about here the passengers who have been on deck eagerly observing tramp steamers, schooners, bugeyes and other harbor craft realize that evening has stolen on them unawares, and that darkness is fast blotting out the distant shores. But inside the boat there is plenty of light and activity, and downstairs in the dining room a hot chicken supper awaits appetites sharpened by salt sea breezes.*

*Oliver Martin, *The Chesapeake and Potomac Country*, published by the C & P Telephone Co. in 1928.

The 1904 fire . . . . A 13-block wide area of downtown Baltimore was laid in ruins by fire on February 7, 1904. The Pratt Street wharves and the buildings on them were destroyed, and only a valiant fire-fighting effort kept the inferno from spreading to Fells Point. Smoke rises from the ashes in this panorama by J. William Schaefer. Even those buildings shown standing were gutted. A giant reconstruction effort got underway immediately.

Rebuilding the docks . . . . The present-day configuration of the Pratt Street wharves is the result of reconstruction after the 1904 fire. Here workers drive pilings for Pier 3, present site of the Aquarium. The tug *Baltimore* is in the foreground of this 1906 photo.   MARYLAND HISTORICAL SOCIETY

MARYLAND HISTORICAL SOCIETY

This view looks up Gay Street from Pier 3, in the opposite direction of the photo on the preceding page. The Custom House can be seen under construction. The building was begun before the fire, and work was able to continue afterwards.

PEALE MUSEUM

MARYLAND HISTORICAL SOCIETY

The watermelon boats . . . . Until recent years, produce boats were a familiar sight alongside the power plant pier, known as Long Dock. The boats brought oysters from the Bay, watermelons from the Eastern Shore, vegetables from Curtis Bay truck gardens. They helped service Market Place just to the north.

To old-timers, the area was known as "Marsh Market," harking back to the days when the market area was filled in over the Jones Falls marsh. A wholesale fish market remained until the 1980s, when the markets gave way to movie theaters and a retail/office complex called The Brokerage.

MARYLAND HISTORICAL SOCIETY

SMITHSONIAN INSTITUTION

Pratt Street was long a receiving center for Chesapeake Bay produce . . . . Here bugeyes, pungies, sloops and schooners cluster at the old piers about 1890.

MARYLAND HISTORICAL SOCIETY

Vegetable waste was once routinely dumped in the reeking harbor . . . This photo, however, may show snow removal. It was taken at the foot of South Street, present site of the Harborplace shopping pavilion, just before the 1904 fire.

MARYLAND HISTORICAL SOCIETY

Unloading Bay craft at Pier 4 . . . . Aquarium mammal theater occupies the pier today.

MARYLAND HISTORICAL SOCIETY

General cargo freighters were a common site at the Pratt Street piers before expansion and modernization of port facilities downriver in the 1950s. . . . Eight large vessels can be counted in this 1948 photo.

Unloading a banana boat.

BALTIMORE GAS & ELECTRIC CO.

The Jones Falls outlet in 1950 . . . . Notice how much the configuration of the piers has changed since the Sachse drawing of 1869. Even though this aerial view is fairly recent, much of what is shown has since vanished. The icebreakers *Annapolis* (left) and *F. C. Latrobe* (right), looking like bugs at their piers, have been scrapped. The firehouse at the end of the pier on the left burned May 16, l980.

The pier on the right is now nothing but pilings. Inland, all of the sheds in the middle of the picture, built out from the old Pennsylvania Railroad President Street Station, have disappeared. The small building just below the sewage pumping station is also gone. It housed the city morgue. The Public Works Museum "streetscape" was erected on the site in l982.

MARYLAND
HISTORICAL
SOCIETY
PHOTOS

Another *Annapolis*, this one a passenger steamer, operated out of Baltimore. Here men from the fireboat *Cataract* tend a blaze aboard her in 1931.

Belching smoke and soot, the *Annapolis* helps a small tanker move through the winter ice in 1942 . . . Icebreaking is an annual chore on Chesapeake Bay. According to one old-timer, the winter of 1918-19 was the worst. "We had a battleship breaking ice all through the Bay and 10 miles out to sea. All we went was two miles a day."

MARYLAND HISTORICAL SOCIETY

The icebreaker *F. C. Latrobe* carried excursionists in the summertime . . . . This group is passing by Federal Hill about 1893.

LAURA F. BROWN

MARYLAND HISTORICAL SOCIETY PHOTOS

When the steamboats died, the Inner Harbor almost died with them . . . . Above, the harbor as it looked in 1948, in the last days of the steamboat era. Mayor Thomas D'Alesandro Jr. had the rotting Light Street piers torn down in 1950. The street was widened, and the Sam Smith waterside park was created on a 200-wide strip of landfill. The overnight Norfolk steamers had their base shifted to Pratt Street, where they continued to operate until 1962. The view below was taken in 1967. In 1970 another 100 feet were added to the western shoreline, consisting of rock and granite behind seawalls, and an additional 30 feet were added out over the water on pylon structures to create the promenade one sees today.

SUNPAPERS

A port for the people . . . . Baltimore's Inner Harbor waterfront is now devoted exclusively to public activities—shopping, strolling, eating, boating. It is the focal point of the city. Here the tall ship *Danmark* pays a visit in 1981.

ROBERT F. KNIESCHE—MARYLAND HISTORICAL SOCIETY COLLECTION

Chapter 11

Fells Point

(Map, p. 68)

FELLS Point was Baltimore's deep-draft ocean port of the 18th and 19th centuries. This waterfront community was born in the age of sail, and her world reknowned shipyards helped bring that age to perfection. The ships and shipyards are gone now, but sailors still find their way to the noisy Greek dancehall bars on lower Broadway. The Seaman's Port Mission is still the community hall. The old Anchorage Hotel, the seaman's YMCA, has been reincarnated as the Admiral Fell Inn. Visitors walking the waterfront square at the foot of Broadway find an authentic maritime flavor. Tugboats whistle and wheeze from their base at Recreation Pier. A marine artifacts store displays objects from around the world. Restaurants with such names as

Fells Point waterfront, about 1941.

Bertha's, Waterfront Hotel, Admiral's Cup, and bars like the Cat's Eye, Dead End, Whistling Oyster and The Horse You Came In On serve a diverse clientele. Food stalls in the two buildings of the Broadway Market cater to the neighborhood and are not as "pricey" as those at Harborplace. When the harbor shuttle boats began serving Fells Point in 1982, shoppers found bargains that helped make up for the cost of the boat ride.

William Fell, an English carpenter and shipwright, purchased over 1,000 acres of land here between 1730 and 1745. His son, Edward, laid off the town of Fells Point in 1763, giving it the English street names found today: Thames (pronounced as it is spelled), Lancaster, Bond, Fleet, Shakespeare, and such colorfully named alleys as Strawberry, Apple, Happy and Petticoat.

Waterfront lots were snapped up quickly for development of wharves, warehouses and shipyards. Access to tracts of white oak, locust and red cedar made Fells Point a natural center for shipbuilding. Deep water made it a terminus for maritime commerce. The community was annexed to Baltimore Town in 1773, about five years after the latter had replaced Joppa, Maryland, as county seat. The community grew rapidly over the next several decades. Saloons and dance halls sprang up, and prostitutes took over the hook of land at the west end, a circumstance to which some historians attribute the origin of the term "hooker."

119

The "point" of Fells Point is at the tip of the old hook, on the choice real estate freed up in 1985 by the closing of the Allied Chemical chrome plant. The chrome operation went back more than a century and a half. In 1845 Isaac Tyson, Jr., established the Baltimore Chrome Works on the north side of the hook, using local chrome ore to manufacture chromium chemicals used in paint, dye and tanning. For more than a decade Tyson controlled the world market. Then high grade ore was found abroad, destroying his monopoly and forcing him to import. Mutual Chemical of New York took over the plant in 1908, and enlarged it several times to keep up with the expanding uses of chromium, including steel production. Allied Chemical and Dye Corp. acquired it in 1954 and operated it for three decades, finally succumbing to foreign competition.

East of the chrome works, one found the decaying piers of Chase's Wharf, Jacksons's Wharf, Brown's Wharf and Henderson's Wharf, which had their heyday in the 1800s, thriving on the flour, coffee and tobacco trades. They were used for general cargo into the present century; another old wharf, Belt's, remained a busy warehouse until developers took over in 1987. Chase's and Henderson's Wharves served the B & O, Jackson's served the Pennsylvania, and Brown's, built in 1822, was used by the Western Maryland. As at Canton and the base of Federal Hill, canneries sprang up among the docks, shipyards and warehouses to handle incoming produce.

Loss of the coffee trade to New York, and the introduction of larger ships requiring deeper water and longer piers, signalled the doom of Fells Point as a port. The last coffee clipper unloaded at Brown's

PHOTO BY AUTHOR

Stevens Dana Bunker, proprietor of the North Atlantic & Orient Trading Co., outside his Fells Point marine artifacts store in 1982.

THOMAS LOISEAUX—NANCY HACKERMAN PRODUCTIONS

Foot of Broadway, 1981, with Brown's Wharf and city pier in foreground.

Wharf in 1890. Prior to World War II, lumber schooners stopped bringing their loads to Lancaster Street yards, giving way to trucks.

During the 1930s intercoastal freight services operated out of Fells Point, Lykes Lines using Henderson's Wharf and Southern Pacific Steamship Lines using Jackson's Wharf. This activity also ended with the outbreak of World War II when the Federal Maritime Commission took over the vessels By the late 1980s, most of the old brick warehouses had undergone a facelift and the shoreline was springing back to life, with shops, restaurants and apartments replacing the departed commercial firms.

Alexander Brown came to Baltimore from Ireland in 1800 and founded what has become one of the world's foremost investment houses . . . . He built his fortune on imports and shipping. By 1825 he operated a fleet of 11 vessels. His son, George, acquired the Brown's Wharf complex in 1840.

BALTIMORE BIOGRAPHY

121

PHOTO BY AUTHOR

Allied Chemical's Fells Point chrome works dominated the entrance to the Inner Harbor . . . . It was the largest multi-purpose chrome plant in the world, employing 400 persons. The plant produced chrome chemicals for use in paint, dye, leather-tanning, chrome-plating, lumber preservation, solar heat panels and video tape. The plant also produced 70 percent of Maryland's hazardous waste, posing, after its closure, one of the most difficult cleanup problems the state has ever faced. Sunken yacht in foreground is the 50-year-old *Felicia*, once owned by the Association of Maryland Pilots. Its steel hull flooded and sank during the harsh winter of 1981-82.

Around the bend from the chrome works, just before Chase's Wharf, is the site of this marine railway which was operated by blacks . . . . It was organized by Isaac Myers, a free-born Baltimore black caulker, in 1866 and operated until its lease was reclaimed in 1884. Several decades earlier, black abolitionist Frederick Douglass worked as a ships carpenter in Fells Point.

PEALE MUSEUM

MARYLAND HISTORICAL SOCIETY

Lumber has long been a major business in Fells Point. In the schooner days, it was unloaded by hand, board by board, as the above photo shows. Vessels laid at dock many days while their cargoes were transferred . . . . At right, the "ram" *B. P. Gravenor* passes Sparrows Point with a load of lumber. Rams were bulky, straight-sided schooners, with dimensions that allowed passage through canals at either end of the Bay . . . . Below, B & O's terminal at Chase's Wharf, which received lumber into the 1940s. The barge at left, the *B. S. Ford*, was a former passenger steamer, converted to bring lumber from the Carolinas. The building with the B & O sign is an old coffee warehouse, still standing. The large building in the distance at the right is Henderson's Wharf, another B & O terminal. Gutted by fire in 1984, it was recycled to become a hotel/office/marina complex.

ENOCH PRATT FREE LIBRARY

MARYLAND HISTORICAL SOCIETY

Tugboat Captain Samuel J. White directs the docking of a tanker at a ship repair yard in 1947 . . . . Much of the work of tugboats involves shifting "dead" ships. Signals are given from the bridge by whistle, hand signals or radio, and the tugs alongside acknowledge each command by repeating the signal. The number of tugs required to place a ship alongside its pier depends entirely on the weather. Without wind, a ship can be handled by one tug. In strong wind it can take up to eight, particularly if the ship is heavily loaded. The captain shown here regarded ship launching as the hardest job. "They go down the way at the time set regardless of weather and we have to dock them."

MARYLAND HISTORICAL SOCIETY

The community life of Fells Point centers around the shops, offices, taverns and play-houses at the foot of Broadway . . . . Across Thames Street, tugboats cluster at the city dock and Recreation Pier, awaiting orders.

PHOTO BY AUTHOR

The first modern-day *Pride of Baltimore* was built in the Inner Harbor and commissioned by the city in 1977 to serve as goodwill ambassador and port promoter. The 90-foot vessel traveled more than 125,000 miles in her nine-year life, visiting ports from the Great Lakes to the West Coast, South America and Europe. She was tragically lost in a freak windstorm off Puerto Rico on May 14, 1986. Capt. Armin Elsaesser, who took this photo, and three others perished. A successor ship, *Pride of Baltimore II*, was launched in 1988.

The Baltimore Clipper

OF ALL the sailing craft developed on Chesapeake Bay, none attracted more attention worldwide than the Baltimore "clipper." These swift vessels emerged at the time of the American Revolution and played a decisive role in the War of 1812. Fells Point was the center of their development.

The Baltimore clipper was a relatively small boat, usually 75-100 feet on deck, lightly built and generously canvassed. Her sharp bow and V-shaped bottom allowed for maximum hull speed, while her tall masts and schooner sail rig enabled her to sail within about 60 degrees of the direction of the wind. Because of these features she could outdist-

ance and outmaneuver most other vessels of her time.

During the War of 1812, Baltimore clippers roamed the Atlantic and Caribbean as "privateers"—privately-owned vessels armed and manned at their owners' expense for the purpose of capturing and destroying enemy merchant craft in time of war. By posting bond to assure adherence to rules and regulations, the ships obtained a government commission, called letter of marque.

Most famous of the clippers was the *Chasseur*, launched by the Thomas Kemp shipyard, Washington and Aliceanna streets, Dec. 12, 1812. "She sat as light and buoyant on the water as a graceful

MARYLAND HISTORICAL SOCIETY

The ultimate clipper, the largest (143 feet) and one of the fastest and most beautiful sailing vessels ever built in the world, was the *Ann McKim*, launched at the Kennard & Williamson yard, Philpot and Point streets, on June 4, 1833 . . . . Baltimore merchant Isaac McKim spared no expense constructing this vessel, which carried flour around the Horn to Peru, returning with copper ore. She carried a "ship" rig, so was unique in her design, possibly influencing the larger "American clipper" that was to come a decade or two later. The *Ann McKim* had the one drawback common to the Baltimore clipper: inadequate cargo capacity for economical peacetime operation. Because of this handicap, the Baltimore clippers eventually gave way to larger ships.

swan," wrote one admirer.

Chasseur captured 11 vessels on her first transatlantic voyage, under Capt. William Wade. On her second major voyage, in 1814 under Capt. Thomas Boyle, she conducted an audacious single-ship "blockade" of the entire English coast. She captured 14 merchant vessels and embarrassed the British Admiralty. A third expedition brought additional successes in the Caribbean as the war ended, and *Chasseur* returned to Baltimore in 1815 in triumph. She was hailed as the "Pride of Baltimore."

When hard times fell after the War of 1812, Fells Point shipping interests found a new use for the Baltimore clippers and a new source of work for the shipyards: adaption of the vessels for use as slavers. The Congress of Vienna outlawed the international slave trade in 1816, and only the swiftest vessels could elude the British fleets posted off Africa to enforce the treaty. The Baltimore clipper was an ideal vessel for this sordid mission. Platforms were installed in the already cramped space below decks and the human cargo was packed in "spoon fashion;" many died during the voyage. A historian wrote in 1941: "the decline of the Baltimore clipper and her gradual perversion to unworthy ends is perhaps the most melancholy chapter in all the history of Baltimore."*

*Hamilton Owens, *Baltimore on the Chesapeake*, Doubleday, Doran & Company, Inc., Garden City, N. Y., 1941.

Letitia Stocket recalled the mood of the clipper ship days in her book, "Baltimore: A Not So Serious History," published in 1928:*

If in your imagination you will clear away the railroad terminals, the practical and no doubt excellent docks on Fells Point, you will be able to re-create the old Point as she was in those clipper days. Up the river, gliding as proudly as swans, came ships from China, from Cuba, from Peru. And ever new ships were upon the ways. There was a good reek of tar and paint and oakum. There was the clink of hammer on steel and the smell of shavings. There was a stir of activity, a constant coming and going, the arrival and departure of vessels. To see a ship make ready for a voyage is even today a thrilling sight. But to see a clipper ship get under way was a picture never to be forgotten. Everywhere on deck and in the rigging there was hurry and excitement, the creak of ropes and the rattle of chains. Voices shouted orders sprinkled liberally with sulpher and brimstone. But over and above the hubbub rose the voice of the chanty man, the leader of the songs, without which no clipper was complete. Often the chanty man was drunk but that made him troll the merrier:
    'In eighteen hundred and forty-six
    I found myself in a hell of a fix'—
and the *Shooting Star* is off to the Horn!

*The Norman, Remington Co., Baltimore.

MARYLAND HISTORICAL SOCIETY

The American clipper was a vessel of the 1850s spurred by the discovery of gold in California in 1848 and Australia in 1851 . . . . A primary requisite for these ships was the ability to carry cargo around the treacherous Cape Horn. Fourteen of these handsome clippers were built in Fells Point in the 1850s. *Flora Temple* was the largest, at 1,916 tons. Fastest was the *Mary Whitridge*, shown here, built by Hunt & Wagner, Fells Street south of Thames, in 1855. Her first passage that year, from Cape Henry to the English Channel, 2,962 miles, in 12 days and 7 hours, was never equalled by any sailing vessel.

Pungy *Wave*, a frequent visitor to Baltimore . . . . Fixed-keel schooners called pungys were direct descendents of the Baltimore clippers. They were the first oyster dredging boats on Chesapeake Bay. Their keel construction made them less practical than the centerboard bugeyes and skipjacks in shallow waters. They eventually disappeared.

MARYLAND HISTORICAL SOCIETY

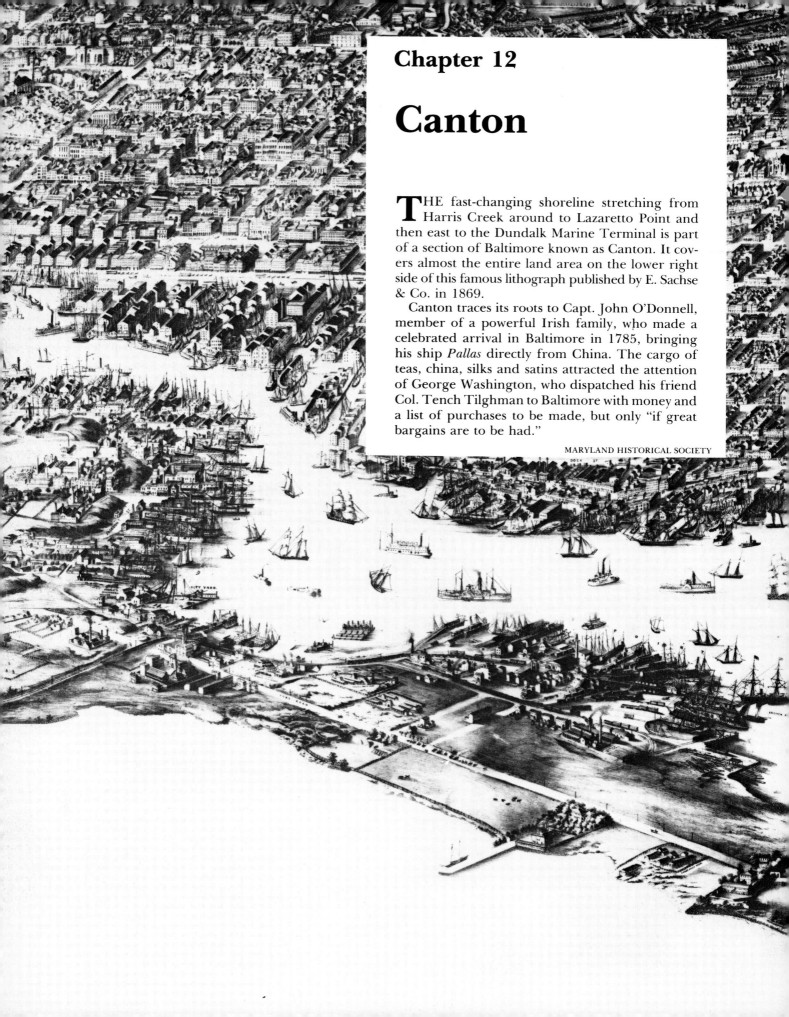

Chapter 12

Canton

THE fast-changing shoreline stretching from Harris Creek around to Lazaretto Point and then east to the Dundalk Marine Terminal is part of a section of Baltimore known as Canton. It covers almost the entire land area on the lower right side of this famous lithograph published by E. Sachse & Co. in 1869.

Canton traces its roots to Capt. John O'Donnell, member of a powerful Irish family, who made a celebrated arrival in Baltimore in 1785, bringing his ship *Pallas* directly from China. The cargo of teas, china, silks and satins attracted the attention of George Washington, who dispatched his friend Col. Tench Tilghman to Baltimore with money and a list of purchases to be made, but only "if great bargains are to be had."

MARYLAND HISTORICAL SOCIETY

Capt. O'Donnell decided to settle in Baltimore. By the time of his death in 1805 he had amassed an estate of 2,500 acres. He called it Canton, apparently in honor of the Chinese city whose goods constributed to his wealth. In 1827, his son Columbus, along with New York capitalist and inventor Peter Cooper and others, formed the Canton Company, with the object of bringing commercial development to the Canton estate and adjoining acreage. Essentially a real estate operation, the company was authorized to lay out streets and build wharves, factories and houses, with the hope of capitalizing on the success of the Baltimore and Ohio Railroad. As it turned out, Canton became the Baltimore terminus of the Pennsylvania Railroad (now Conrail), and for about 50 years in the present century the Canton Company was owned by that railroad.

Canton has been a source of many fortunes. The initial Canton Co. stock became a fad on Wall Street—some thought it was in China—and, according to the Baltimore *Sun*, its early promoters were not averse to holding "rigged" land sales in order to "puff and inflate the price of the stock." Pennsylvania Railroad's holding company paid $15 million for the Canton Co. in 1929, collected handsome dividends over the next three decades, then, in 1960, sold the company to International Mining Co., a New York-based conglomerate. The railroad kept substantial waterfront holdings for itself, including its general cargo and coal and grain piers.

Even with its holdings thus reduced to 184 acres, Canton Co. continued to be the largest private marine terminal operator on the East Coast. For another two decades it carried on a range of activities from terminal facilities on the main river east of Lazaretto Point, where piers were equipped to handle ore, bananas, containers, vehicles and general cargo. The Canton Railroad, a small road started by the company in 1906, connected the piers with industrial plants in northeast Baltimore.

In 1977, Pacific Holding Co. purchased International Mining and Pacific was subsequently acquired by the Murdock Development Corp. of California, making Murdock owners of the Canton Co. In September 1980, the Murdock interests resold a portion of the Canton holdings, including Canton Railroad and the piers, to Consolidation Coal Sales Co. for development into a major East Coast coal-loading pier. The first coal trains arrived at the terminal in 1983—just as the bottom fell out of the world market. Meanwhile, the Canton Co., 150 years old in 1978, continued to operate some scattered holdings from the Murdock offices in the World Trade Center.

Peter Cooper founded the Boston Street iron works shown in the Sachse lithograph, using ore dug at Lazaretto Point. A man of many accomplishments, Cooper built the *Tom Thumb* in 1829 to prove that a steam railroad engine could go around the short curves in the existing B & O line and that the railroad was therefore a viable operation with a promising future.

Cooper sold his iron works to Horace Abbott, who took on the assignment at the time of the Civil War of furnishing protective iron plates for the federal gunship *Monitor*. He completed the task ahead of schedule and in time for her to engage the *Merrimac* in Hampton Roads and save the wooden fleet of the U.S. Navy. The action influenced the outcome of the war and opened a new era in naval architecture.

MARYLAND HISTORICAL SOCIETY

A LONG the Canton waterfront, the new is superimposed, and the old is seldom totally erased. Visible traces remain that carry the observer far back into Baltimore, and American, history.

This air view, looking east along Boston Street in 1952, shows Canton at the peak of its commercial and industrial activity. A number of the buildings shown here have since been leveled or abandoned.

The section of Boston Street in the foreground was known as "Canners Row." Many of the buildings were erected here to handle produce brought in by the sailing fleet: oysters from the Bay, vegetables from the Eastern Shore, pineapples from the Bahamas. A 130-foot clipper ship was found buried here in 1908, 400 feet inland from the present shoreline. It had been burned at its pier.

In the present century the American Can Company built the large complex which manufactured cans on the north side of Boston Street, on the triangular tract formerly occupied by the Abbot iron works. Beyond the can factory is the community of Canton, marked by the twin towers of St. Casimer's Church on O'Donnell Street.

American can straddled the remains of Harris Creek, whose outlet is marked by a concrete viaduct under Boston Street. On the west bank of this creek in 1797, shipwright David Stodder turned out the U.S. Frigate *Constellation*, still afloat as a museum in Baltimore's Inner Harbor (page 97).

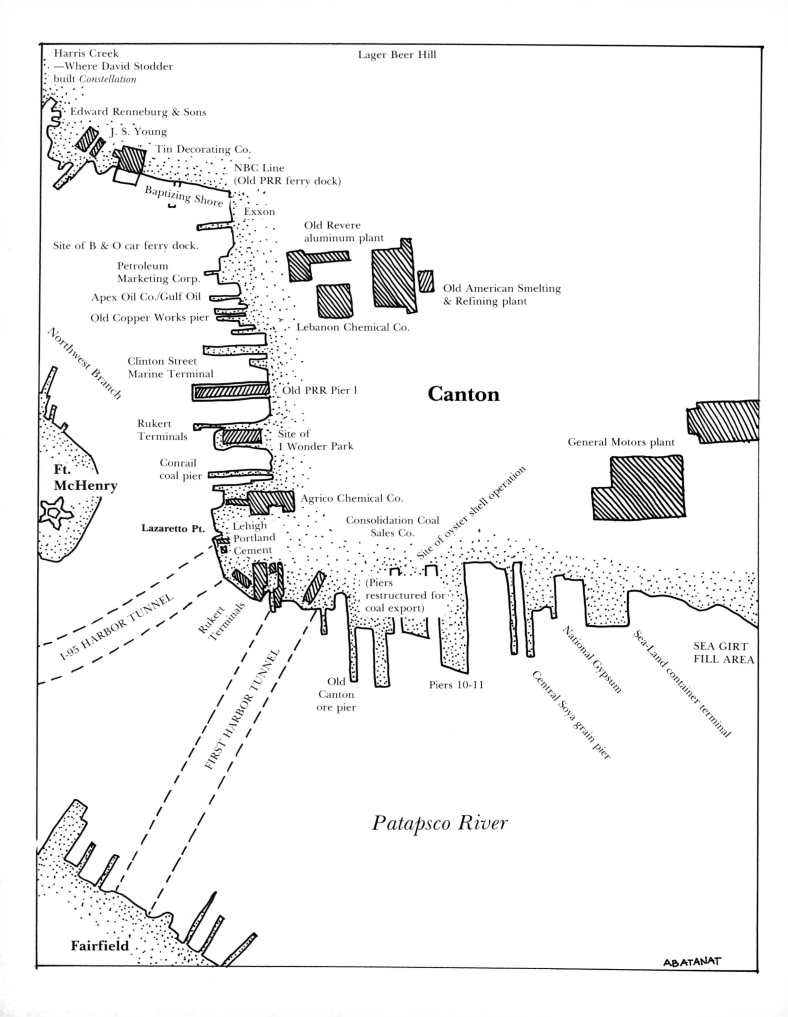

Harris Creek
—Where David Stodder
built *Constellation*

Lager Beer Hill

Edward Renneburg & Sons

J. S. Young

Tin Decorating Co.

Baptizing Shore

NBC Line
(Old PRR ferry dock)

Exxon

Old Revere
aluminum plant

Site of B & O car ferry dock.

Petroleum
Marketing Corp.

Apex Oil Co./Gulf Oil

Old Copper Works pier

Old American Smelting
& Refining plant

Lebanon Chemical Co.

Northwest Branch

Clinton Street
Marine Terminal

Old PRR Pier 1

Canton

Rukert
Terminals

Site of
I Wonder Park

**Ft.
McHenry**

Conrail
coal pier

General Motors plant

Agrico Chemical Co.

Lazaretto Pt.

Lehigh
Portland
Cement

Consolidation Coal
Sales Co.

Site of oyster shell operation

I-95 HARBOR TUNNEL

Rukert
Terminals

(Piers
restructured for
coal export)

FIRST HARBOR TUNNEL

Old
Canton
ore pier

Piers 10-11

Central Soya grain pier

National Gypsum

Sea-Land container terminal

SEA GIRT
FILL AREA

Patapsco River

Fairfield

ABATANAT

BALTIMORE: TWO HUNDREDTH ANNIVERSARY

THE 1980s saw the transformation of "Canners Row" into Baltimore's new "Gold Coast." Waterfront town houses replaced the old Boston Street canneries. Plans were laid for a major yachting center east of Harris Creek, along with shops and apartments incorporating existing historic buildings. One of these, constructed on the site of the old Booz shipyard, was originally a chair factory. It was occupied from 1912 to 1985 by Edward Renneburg & Sons Co, which fabricated steel plates and machinery, including special equipment for the local canning industry and the Chesapeake menhaden fishery.

East of the old Renneburg factory were large buildings occupied by J.S. Young & Co., manufacturer of licorice (for flavoring tobacco), dyes and tanning extracts. The factory was served by some of the last four-masted schooners on the Bay, bringing logwood from the Caribbean to provide substances required in dye-making. By 1987 the old Young buildings had been reincarnated as Boatel Baltimore, and architects were at work to transform the American Can site across Boston Street.

East of the Young plant, at the foot of Kenwood, was the Baltimore Lumber Co. and Chesapeake Marine Railway Co., which were destroyed by an 18-alarm, $5 million fire in February 1951.

The large, solid building east of the licorice plant, with its own power plant on the water, was the home of the Tin Decorating Co. of Baltimore, one of the world's largest manufacturers of lithographed tin packages and boxes. It could produce 5 million colorful boxes a day. The building had a rebirth in 1986 as Tindeco Wharf, one of the city's most prestigious new residential addresses.

The park site to the east was leased from 1979 until 1985 by the Norfolk, Baltimore & Carolina (NBC) Line, which used World War II landing ships to provide overnight container shipping service to

First location of Booz Bros. shipyard in Baltimore, at Canton around 1875 . . . . The steambox at center was used for softening timbers and the mold loft at right was for laying down full size patterns. Beyond the mold loft can be seen the old bridge over Harris Creek. The Booz yard was moved to Federal Hill in 1879.

PEALE MUSEUM

Philadelphia and Norfolk. The line was founded in 1922 and operated from downtown until its piers were needed for Inner Harbor development. NBC's unglamorous but efficient freight handling methods provided stiff competition for the Old Bay Line and helped put the latter out of business.

The Exxon facility, at the turn of the shoreline, traces its beginnings to 1868 when the Canton Oil Works was established on this site to refine crude oil from Pennsylvania into fuel oils, grease and wax. The lighter materials, naptha and gasoline, were considered waste at the time, and were drained into ponds and burned. Initially the oil was brought in by cattle car in barrels, but in 1883 a pipeline was opened from the Pennsylvania fields; this was eventually extended to Oklahoma. In 1892, the refinery, then called Baltimore United Oil Co., was purchased by Standard Oil. The wharves were a colorful sight in the early 1900s when three magnificent oil sailers—steel-hulled four-masted barques—were chartered by Standard Oil to carry oil and kerosene from Canton to the Far East, returning with tea or manganese ore. The *Daylight* (3,756 tons), *Arrow* and *Eclipse* (3,090 tons each) gave way to steamers at the beginning of World War I.

In 1913, with the opening of the Panama Canal, crude oil was brought to Baltimore by water, from California and Mexico. The pipeline was discontinued in 1925, and in 1957 the refinery itself was closed. The facility was changed to a storage and distribution center exclusively. Today Exxon tankers arrive regularly with refined products from Aruba in the West Indies to supply local needs.

The oil docks mask two unrelated early uses of this shoreline. The old Canton Race Track, at Clinton and Boston streets, was the site of the 1840 Whig Convention where Henry Clay orated and William Henry Harrison was nominated for the Presidency. And the foot of Cardiff Avenue was the site of Baltimore's first public bathing beach, opened in 1893 when workers' homes had no running water for baths. The area became known as "baptizing shore" when several Baptist churches used it for Sunday afternoon ceremonies.

A nearly obliterated pier one block south of Cardiff marks the terminus of a B & O railroad ferry service that connected Canton with Locust Point in the 1880s and symbolized the rivalry between B & O and the Pennsylvania. At the time of the Civil War, B & O monopolized rail transportation between Washington, D.C. and Baltimore, and riders to or from the north had to make a cumbersome connection between B & O's Camden Station and the President Street station of the Philadelphia, Wilmington and Baltimore Railroad, the Pennsylvania's predecessor. All this changed in the 1870s with the completion of two cross-town tunnels: on the east side, the Canton Co. built the Hoffman Street tunnel to improve rail service to its piers; and on the west side, Pennsylvania Railroad interests built the Baltimore & Potomac tunnel under Wilson Street, ostensibly as a route to southern Maryland but with a "spur" to Washington that enabled the Pennsy to outflank B & O and break its monopoly. By running trains through the two new tunnels, the Pennsylvania affiliates inaugu-

Unloading bananas at Canton, 1963.

MARYLAND HISTORICAL SOCIETY

ROBERT F. KNIESCHE—MARYLAND HISTORICAL SOCIETY COLLECTION

John Williams laid out this half-acre park across from his Clinton Street tavern in 1901
. . . . It became known as I Wonder Park and was popular with dock workers. Williams
used goats to maintain the park and someone donated six mulberry trees. But then the
Maritime Commission built an office and warehouse on the grounds in 1941, and I
Wonder Park was no more. The site was at 2100 South Clinton Street. The little cars of
the Conrail coal-loading pier can be seen in the background.

rated through passenger service, New York and Philadelphia to Washington, in June 1873. The same tunnels, antiquated and beset by cracks and leaks, are used by Amtrak today.

In 1886, B & O extended its own service to Philadelphia by way of Canton, using the ferries *John W. Garrett* and *Canton* to transport whole trains across from Locust Point. The ferries were B & O's only north-south link until 1895 when the railroad completed the present-day Howard Street tunnel connecting Camden station with the station at Mt. Royal to the north, which connected in turn with the line to Philadelphia. Passenger service on this line was discontinued in the late 1950s and the unneeded Mt. Royal station was turned over to the Maryland Institute for use as an arts school.

In 1850, the Baltimore Copper Smelting Co. was established on South Clinton Street alongside the B & O line. Within a decade it became the largest smelting operation of its kind in the United States, importing ore from Chile and Cuba, and contributing to the wealth of Baltimore's famous childless entrepreneurs, Johns Hopkins and Enoch Pratt, whose philanthrophy ultimately provided the city with a university, hospital, medical school and system of free public libraries. The successor to this

19th century operation, American Smelting and Refining Co., closed its doors in 1975 and moved to Texas, idling a large physical plant one block inland from the waterfront, and adding to the desolation created when Revere Aluminum closed its plant just to the north in 1967. One reason for American Smelting's move was the prohibitive cost of bringing the old plant into compliance with modern standards for its discharges into the Patapsco. Cardiff Avenue remains as a reminder of the skilled Welsh copper workers employed in the early days. The copper works pier, just south of the foot of Eastbourne Ave., can be identified by the narrow guage iron tracks meandering over from the old refinery.

Further south on Clinton Street is the old Pier 1 of the Pennsylvania Railroad. This major pier, with four ship berths for general cargo, is now operated by the Maryland Port Adminstration and served by Conrail.

South of Pier 1 is the Pier 5 complex of Rukert Terminals Corp. Rukert specializes in unloading odd bulk cargoes which other terminals can't or won't handle. The facilities include another two-acre terminal just down Clinton Street at Lazaretto Point. The Rukert operation had its start in 1921

This spectacular fire July 17, 1932 destroyed Pennsylvania Railroad Piers 2, 3 and 4 and severely damaged Pier 1. The piers were rebuilt two years later.

MARYLAND HISTORICAL SOCIETY

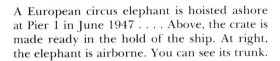

A European circus elephant is hoisted ashore at Pier 1 in June 1947 . . . . Above, the crate is made ready in the hold of the ship. At right, the elephant is airborne. You can see its trunk.

MARYLAND
HISTORICAL
SOCIETY
PHOTOS

when Capt. W. G. N. Rukert, with a dream and an unsecured loan of $800, purchased a second hand truck and rented a garage downtown. In 1930, with the help of Willoughby McCormick, founder of McCormick & Co., "Cap" Rukert purchased some docks in Fells Point, and over the next several decades he obtained historic Brown's Wharf in Fells Point as well as the properties along Clinton Street in Canton. His son, Norman, took over the presidency in 1961, distinguishing himself meanwhile by the writing and publication of port histories. His *Historic Canton* was an important source for portions of this chapter. Mr. Rukert was active in the Maryland Historical Society and operated a small maritime museum at Brown's Wharf. He died in 1984.

In 1878, Bernard N. Baker and James C. Whitely formed a partnership to supply bunker coal to ships. Their 400-foot trestle pier was fed with wooden drop-bottom cars. A later version, built on the same site in 1917 by the Pennsylvania Railroad, was 1,100 feet long and could handle 900 tons an hour, enabling Baltimore to become the East Coast's leading coaling station before oil replaced coal as the primary ship fuel.

South of the coal pier is the fertilizer pier of Agrico Chemical Co., descendent of the American Agricultural Chemical Co., which was an amalgum of several companies put together by the "fertilizer trust" around the turn of the century when Baltimore was the nation's center for fertilizer production. For many years the plant here was the city's largest. It was known originally as the Lazaretto Guano Works, after the raw material imported from Peru. Production shifted to manufacture from bone meal, then to synthetics. Now the plant barges in phosphates and nitrogen from Louisiana and Florida and distributes the material to customers for their own custom blending. Fertilizer manufacture continues to be carried out by the Lebanon Chemical Co. to the south, which took over the old Baugh/ Kerr McGee chemical works in 1979.

MARYLAND HISTORICAL SOCIETY

Lazaretto Point in 1872. Ad, below, shows another view about the same year.

MARYLAND HISTORICAL SOCIETY

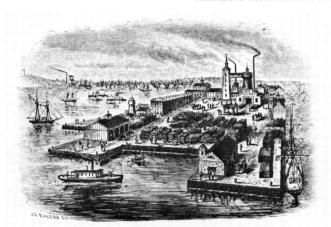

STICKNEY IRON COMPANY,
CLINTON STREET, CANTON.
CHARCOAL PIG IRON.

J. H. STICKNEY, PRESIDENT.　　WILLIAM OLIVER, JR., MANAGER.
WILLIAM HARVEY, SECRETARY.　　REED, STICKNEY & CO., SELLING AGENTS.

OFFICE,—No. 42 SECOND STREET,

BALTIMORE.

LEHIGH Portland Cement Co.'s tall storage towers mark Canton's most historic spot, Lazaretto Point, where a lighthouse was an important city landmark for 125 years. Originally called Gorsuch Point, it was a source of iron ore for the Principio Furnace Co. in the early 1700s, and for Peter Cooper's iron works a century later.

Around 1801 an isolation hospital for smallpox victims was built here and the point took on the name "Lazaretto" which means fever hospital or pesthouse in Italian. In 1831, a 34-foot-high round brick lighthouse was built near the hospital to guide harbor traffic. The light was used to demonstrate the new Fresnel lenses in 1852 and in 1916 was the first lighthouse in Maryland and Virginia to be electrified. But the growth of piers and fertilizer factories caused the view of the light to be blocked, so in 1926 the famous old landmark was demolished and a steel tower erected in its place 100 yards closer to the water.

In 1870 the smallpox quarantine operation was moved to Curtis Bay (see page 31). After that, the Coast Guard used the lighthouse site for buoy-tending operations. In 1954 the light on the steel tower itself was turned off because of the interference by surrounding buildings, and in 1958 the Coast Guard moved its buoy operations to its yard on Curtis Creek. In 1962 the 4.2 acre site, with its rotting piers and decayed buildings, was sold to Lehigh Cement for $175,000.

MARYLAND HISTORIAL SOCIETY

Lazaretto Point in use as a Coast Guard buoy depot in 1939 . . . . The old two-story quarantine building and small house, both depicted in the lithographs at left, are still standing in this photo, but the lighthouse is gone. The steel tower which replaced it casts a shadow beside ship at center of picture.

PHOTO BY AUTHOR

All traces of the Lazeretto station have disappeared in this 1982 photo. Cement towers cover the lighthouse site while a temporary trench is cut at right for the laying of the new highway tunnel. In 1985, after the trench was refilled, the Rukert company erected a replica lighthouse here, as a memorial to their founder and his son.

CONSOLIDATION COAL SALES CO.

East of Lebanon Chemical is one of the world's most modern coal terminals, which replaced old ore and general piers of the Canton Co. in the early 1980s.

The architect's drawing above shows how the complex operates. Arriving rail cars pass through a long low thawing shed in the middle foreground and are then uncoupled in pairs for the rotary dumper, which can handle 50 cars an hour. The coal falls into an underground hopper and then is carried by conveyor to the top of a great silo-like "transfer-sampling station" at middle left. From here it is sent directly out to a waiting ship, or conveyed to the large black storage piles that dominate the center of the drawing. Two gigantic machines called stacker/reclaimers, moving on tracks, have the capability of stacking the arriving coal or reclaiming it from the stacks for shiploading. The facility opened in 1983 and is capable of handling 10 million tons of coal annually. Consolidation Coal Sales Co. paid $30 million for the site (including the Canton Railroad) and invested another $80 million in its conversion to a coal terminal.

The Canton Co. piers have played important roles in port history. The Pier 10-11 complex, shown at right in the drawing, was a major Army supply base for the European Theater in World War II. At Pier 10, Sea-Land Service's S.S. *Mobile* arrived on April 9, 1963, to inaugurate container service between Baltimore and Puerto Rico; this pier became the first in the port to be designated for container freight.

East of these piers is the Canton grain elevator, pictured at right, and beyond the grain elevator is the Sea Girt container terminal, which Sea-Land Service began to develop for its own use in 1965, as its operations proved so successful. The site was the original location of Thompson's Sea Girt Restaurant, famous for fifty-cent fish and chicken dinners. The Sea Girt terminal began to undergo considerable expansion in 1982 as dredge spoil from the new harbor tunnel was pumped in behind a dike and allowed to settle (see photo, page 81).

Inland a mile or so from the docks are such Canton landmarks as the huge General Motors assembly plant, a Lever Brothers plant (purchased from Gold Dust in 1939) where Lux, Lifebuoy, Rinso and Swan are made, and the very visible Lager Beer Hill, where the Canton Co. leased deep cellars to a succession of major local brewers (National, Gunther, Schaefer, Hamm's) since the 1860s.

BALTIMORE GAS & ELECTRIC CO.

Freighters load on each side of the Pennsylvania Railroad grain pier in this 1967 photo . . . . The pier with its 4 million bushel elevator has been a Canton landmark since 1923. It is now operated by Central Soya. Behind the grain pier a third ship can be seen at the dock of National Gypsum Co., which has operated a plant at the foot of Newkirk Street since 1947.

PHOTO BY AUTHOR

Since the end of 1975 the old Grace Line ship *Santa Rosa* has lain idle in Canton . . . . She was purchased at auction for $1 million by Vintero Sales Corp. of New York for refurbishing as a cruise ship, but a series of setbacks, including a five-month shipyard strike, upset the plans. Built in 1959, the 583-foot ship carried 361 passengers on Graces's Latin American run and was one of the finest luxury ships afloat.

ROBERT F. KNIESCHE—MARYLAND HISTORICAL SOCIETY COLLECTION

Bugeye *Russell A. Wingate* and "buyboat" *Louise* unloading at oyster shell plant.

COAL pier construction forced the shutdown of an oyster shell operation initiated in 1911 by the Potomac Poultry Food Corp. The Company, which produced crushed oyster shell for use as a calcium source for laying hens, originally obtained its supply of shells by buying them from shucking operations all over the eastern seaboard and bringing them in boats such as those shown in the picture above.

In the 1950s, the company was purchased by Southern Industries of Mobile, Ala., and renamed Oyster Shell Products Corp. Southern had discovered vast beds of oyster shell in the Gulf of Mexico and speculated that similar reefs could be found in Chesapeake Bay. Their search uncovered large beds, up to 30 feet thick and amounting to millions

of tons, accumulated before man came along to harvest the Bay's product. The shells were anywhere from several hundred up to 5,000 years old, some under ten feet of silt.

In 1960, Southern negotiated arrangements with the State of Maryland and with C. J. Langenfelder & Son, a local company, whereby Langenfelder dredged the old shell reefs, providing shells to the State every spring for reseeding commercial beds, and supplying the Canton company with shells the remainder of the season. Langenfelder set up a base at the old ferry dock at Love Point, across the Bay, accumulating a mountain of oyster shells visible to passing boaters. Langenfelder continued supplying the State and other enterprises following the shutdown of its Canton customer.

On old Point Breeze, at the extreme eastern end of the Canton shoreline, was the Baltimore works of the Western Electric Company, which was closed in the mid-1980s . . . . Riverview Amusement Park, shown below, a Baltimore recreation spot for 30 years, was razed in 1929 to make way for the Bell system plant. The plant employed some 6,500 persons and was a major supplier of insulated cable, producing coaxial cable, armored submarine cable, and thousands of miles of ordinary telephone wire annually. In 1982 the shoreline at upper left was filled in with dredge spoil from the Ft. McHenry tunnel, leaving Point Breeze no longer a distinguishable landmark.

MARYLAND HISTORICAL SOCIETY PHOTOS

MARYLAND HISTORICAL SOCIETY

Dundalk was created out of harbor mud in 1938, serving first as Baltimore's municipal airport . . . . Great flying "clippers" docked on Colgate Creek, taking on passengers for Bermuda, the Caribbean and Europe. But the field itself was a problem. When the top crust hardened, it left muck underneath. Runways wrinkled and buckled when large planes landed. Aviation authorities were glad to give up Harbor Field and move the operation to Friendship Airport (now Baltimore-Washington International) south of the city. The Western Electric plant (p. 143) is at left in these two photos, taken some 30 years apart.

Chapter 13

Dundalk Terminal

BALTIMORE GAS & ELECTRIC CO.

DUNDALK Marine Terminal is the heart of the modern-day Port of Baltimore. Because of its size and scale of operations, it is one of the most interesting and exciting harbor facilities to be found anywhere in the world. For reasons of safety and security, few visitors are ever given an opportunity to observe its fascinations. An imposing ten-lane entrance for arriving trucks only hints at the bustle inside. At water's edge, ten giant container cranes stand as sentinels, welcoming large ships, and piquing the curiosity of occupants of passing small boats. Dundalk Terminal should have a visitors gallery and tour bus, so that the public can see first hand what the Port of Baltimore is all about.

Among other things, Dundalk is a fast-turnaround container terminal. Ships enter, unload their great boxes, take on other boxes and leave, before their arrival can be published in the newspaper. The terminal is also a landing area for Japanese and European autos and other general cargo. Lumber, wire, machinery and other items fill the grounds, along with great stacks of containers. A 140-acre storage area is rented to shipping companies at $23,000 annually per acre. Tracks are provided for trailertrains—railcars bearing containers from the Midwest or as far away as the Pacific Coast.

The Maryland Port Authority purchased the land at Dundalk for $4 million in 1959 as one of that new agency's first steps to modernize the port and make it accessible to truck traffic. Now expanded to some 600 acres, mostly dredge spoil, the facility can handle as many as 13 ships at one time.

DUNDALK-PATAPSCO NECK HISTORICAL SOCIETY

Old swimming hole . . . . These 1920s photos were taken at the Maryland Swimming Club, which flourished on Dundalk Avenue until the shoreline was filled in for Harbor Field. The club was set up in 1903 at the former summer home of the McShane family, who operated a nearby foundry. In 1894, William McShane gave the name Dundalk to the foundry's railroad stop, which was located between St. Helena and Turner Station. During World War I, Bethlehem Steel Co. built the town of Dundalk on two farms near the foundry site, to provide housing for workers at Sparrows Point.

Dundalk and the other ship terminals nearby mean big dollars to Baltimore and the State of Maryland.

Shipowners can spend thousands of dollars on a single port stop. In 1978, the Baltimore *News-American* found it cost nearly $78,000 for the Greek-owned bulk carrier *Samos Glory* to load a grain cargo at Port Covington. This included $5,400 for six days dockage, a $31,300 stevedoring charge for loading the grain, $12,250 for overtime use of the grain elevator, about $3,000 in piloting charges for bringing the ship to and from the mouth of the Bay, $270 each time for line handlers to help dock and undock the ship, about $500 for each use of a tug, and $750 for the services of a local ship agent.

Food, fuel and other stores must be taken on while the ship is in port and this activity nurtures a large marine service industry in Baltimore. One company specializes in fast handling of ships' laundry. Another offers tank barge loads of fresh water. Ship chandlery firms supply rope, wire, anchors, repair parts, and all kinds of other equipment. A Highlandtown chandlery stocks Oriental, Scandinavian, Greek, Italian, British, German and Indian food specialties and has a priest supervise and certify the slaughter of animals for Moslem crews. "A Greek ship wants 30 pounds of feta cheese, a British tramper requests five cases of steak and kidney pies, a Japanese auto carrier orders 75 pints of boiled octopus, a Russian container ship would like five cases of face soap, a Norwegian tanker 300 pounds of lute fish," the same *News-American* article reported.

It is estimated that 79,000 persons are employed in port-related activities. The port is Maryland's largest business, and generates $1 out of every $10 in the economic activity of the state.

Containerships at Dundalk.

BALTIMORE GAS & ELECTRIC CO.

The 'Container Revolution'

ONE factor that helped Baltimore maintain its position as a general cargo port was its early adapatation to the container method of shipping. Containers brought a revolution in ocean shipping over the last two decades, and ports which saw the container as only a fad were left by the wayside.

The potential for containers became evident to Baltimore port planners when Dundalk Terminal was in the development stage. As a former airfield, Dundalk was perfectly suited to handle the big boxes. It had the large open spaces needed to hold them pending ship arrivals. It had "marginal" berths (berths alongside the shore, as opposed to berths at long "finger" piers that characterized railroad terminals), ideal for installation of the huge cranes needed to transfer the boxes between shore and ship and store them in stacks. The wonderful serendipity of Dundalk helped turn Baltimore into the second largest container port on the East and Gulf Coasts, after New York.

The typical ship container is a box of stainless steel and aluminum, either 20 or 40 feet long, eight feet wide and eight feet high, with double doors at one end. It is like a truck van without wheels; in fact, part of the time it *is* a truck van, hauled to or from dockside on a flat bed trailer. The most important aspect of the container is that it is "intermodal," meaning that the same container can be hauled from shipper to customer, via ship, truck or rail, throughout the world.

In the "old" days, that is from the time of the ancient Phoenicians up to about 25 years ago, general cargo (called "breakbulk cargo") was brought to the dock in boxes, bags, cartons, crates, drums or whatever, rolled aboard or hoisted by ship or shoreside crane, and stowed by hand—a slow, tedious process. The container, by contrast, can be loaded at the shipper's factory, and transferred "intermodally" all the way to the recipient—without any need to open the box or rehandle its contents except possibly for random inspection by customs agents.

The containers one sees at a ship terminal may contain almost anything imaginable: rugs, furniture, vehicles, chemicals, bulk liquids, heavy machinery, livestock (some containers are ventilated),

147

perishable commodities (some are refrigerated)—anything that will fit in a box and is of sufficient quantity to justify the container freight rate.

Containers are sped to all parts of the world on ships especially designed to carry them. The ships operate as "liners," i.e. with definite routes and regular published schedules, so that ship line customers can determine how to route their cargoes and when to get them to the docks. Some shippers make these arrangements themselves; others hire specialists called "freight forwarders" to make sure the cargo reaches its destination by the most economical and efficient means.

The container business as we know it is the invention of a North Carolina trucker named Malcolm McLean who bought an old vessel in the mid-1950s and outfitted it so that it could take his truck trailers to sea. He developed a virtual monopoly moving general cargo from New York to Puerto Rico and from the West Coast to Alaska. For nearly a decade, McLean's Sea-Land Service, Inc., was one of the few steamship lines in the world using containerization, but the potential was soon obvious. A standard dock crew of 22 or 23 men could handle

16 times more container tonnage per hour than non-containerized loose cargo. Faster cargo handling meant drastically reduced labor costs per ton handled, and led to other important savings: less time lost at harbor piers, and therefore more trips per vessel; less pier rental; reduced pierside storage charges. The secure, weatherproof containers also brought drastic reductions in pilferage, breakage and weather damage.

The economics involved in the containership's takeover of general cargo shipping were reported by Helen Delich Bentley in the Baltimore *Sun* Dec. 23, 1968. Bentley was describing a settlement between ship owners and the cargo handlers's union, the International Longshoreman's Assn. (AFL-CIO). At the time, she explained, it cost the containership operators $8,000 a day to keep up finance payments on one of their new vessels even if it was laid up at the dock, whereas breakbulk operators, using World War II freighters long since amortized, paid only $300 a day for an idle ship. Faced with such high layup costs, the container operators "will pay labor any price before succumbing to a strike," Bentley wrote. And, for them, the price was not

Anatomy of a containership.

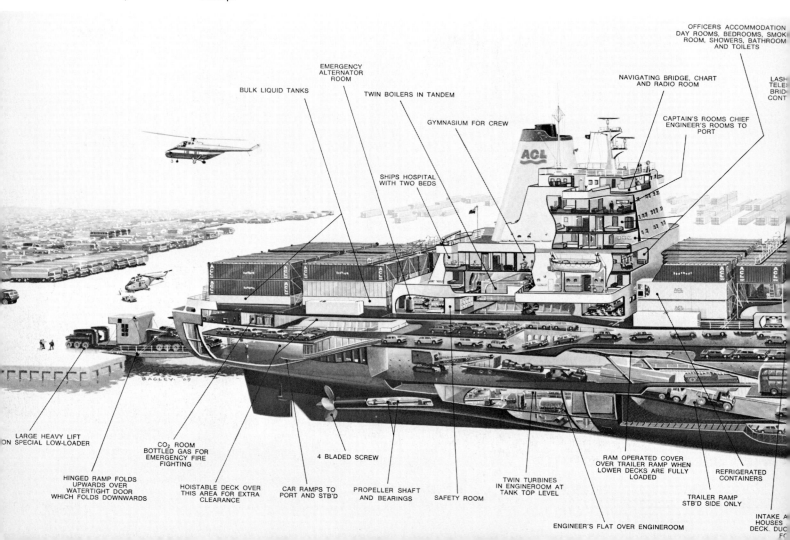

that high. A $1.60 hourly wage increase over three years added only 35 cents a ton to the cost of handling containers, compared to $3 a ton to the cost of handling breakbulk.

Sea-Land Service established a container service between Baltimore and Puerto Rico in 1963, using pier 10 at Canton (see p. 140). The venture was so successful that Sea-Land worked with the Canton Co. to develop the "Sea Girt" terminal, between Canton and Dundalk, especially for Sea-Land's containerships. Sea Girt opened in 1967. Meanwhile, Dundalk Terminal was redesigned to handle container traffic, and her container facilities were expanded in 1973. In 1979 MPA opened a three-berth container terminal at South Locust Point. In 1981 dredge spoil from the new harbor tunnel was pumped to Sea Girt to expand the acreage there. MPA meanwhile purchased land at Masonville, on the south side of Middle Branch near Hanover Street, and announced plans to open a new 350-acre container terminal there in the 1990s. Within a space of 15 years, container traffic moving through the Port of Baltimore grew from almost nothing to over 4 million tons a year.

PHOTO BY AUTHOR

Containership in drydock at Fairfield.

COURTESY ATLANTIC CONTAINER LINES

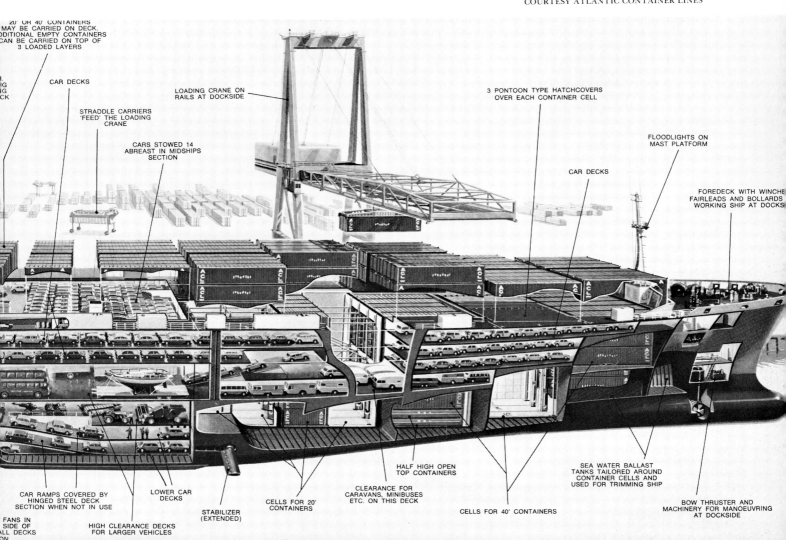

20' OR 40' CONTAINERS MAY BE CARRIED ON DECK. ADDITIONAL EMPTY CONTAINERS CAN BE CARRIED ON TOP OF 3 LOADED LAYERS

CAR DECKS

LOADING CRANE ON RAILS AT DOCKSIDE

3 PONTOON TYPE HATCHCOVERS OVER EACH CONTAINER CELL

STRADDLE CARRIERS 'FEED' THE LOADING CRANE

FLOODLIGHTS ON MAST PLATFORM

CARS STOWED 14 ABREAST IN MIDSHIPS SECTION

CAR DECKS

FOREDECK WITH WINCHES FAIRLEADS AND BOLLARDS WORKING SHIP AT DOCKS

CAR RAMPS COVERED BY HINGED STEEL DECK SECTION WHEN NOT IN USE

LOWER CAR DECKS

HALF HIGH OPEN TOP CONTAINERS

SEA WATER BALLAST TANKS TAILORED AROUND CONTAINER CELLS AND USED FOR TRIMMING SHIP

FANS IN SIDE OF ALL DECKS

HIGH CLEARANCE DECKS FOR LARGER VEHICLES

STABILIZER (EXTENDED)

CELLS FOR 20' CONTAINERS

CLEARANCE FOR CARAVANS, MINIBUSES ETC. ON THIS DECK

CELLS FOR 40' CONTAINERS

BOW THRUSTER AND MACHINERY FOR MANOEUVRING AT DOCKSIDE

BALTIMORE GAS & ELECTRIC CO.

Ore carrier . . . . *Dry bulk* ships, designed for commodities like coal and grain, usually carry no booms; their decks are clear, except for access hatches through which cargo is loaded and unloaded by shore machinery.

MARYLAND HISTORICAL SOCIETY

Breakbulk freighter . . . . These ships carry their own cargo booms; the tall supporting columns are distinctive features.

Types of Ships

A CONTAINERSHIP is easily recognizable from the boxes stacked high on deck, secured in place by guy wires. Several other types of ships stop at Dundalk or at specialized terminals nearby. The most typical are shown on these pages. Some ships combine the features shown here. For instance, many containerships have "RO/RO" ramps for loading vehicles; some ships can carry bulk liquid in one

Ships designed to transport autos, buses, trucks, tractors and similar vehicles are called *RO/RO* ships, meaning "roll-on, roll-off" . . . . The cargo is driven aboard instead of being placed by cranes.

Ramp becomes two-lane highway.

BARBER BLUE SEA LINE

MARYLAND HISTORICAL SOCIETY

Passenger ship . . . . The ocean passenger liner is seldom seen any more in Baltimore. Dundalk has a passenger facility, but it is used only occasionally by cruise ships. The *Constitution*, shown above, was laid up in Baltimore in the early 1970s. It now operates in the Hawaiian Islands.

Oil tanker . . . . These *liquid bulk* ships usually carry a maze of pipes and valves on deck, in place of hatches.

hold, mixed general cargo in another and grain or ore in a third. To a practiced eye, deck equipment quickly reveals a ship's purpose. An interesting game for boaters can be made by checking ships seen against the listing of vessel arrivals in the daily newspaper. This will show not only cargo carried, but where the ship is from, where it is going, and its nation of registry.

A highly specialized ship is the *LASH*, standing for "lighter aboard ship" in which the lighter is a 30-foot by 60-foot barge . . . . In this operation the box-like barge can be towed into shallow waters and up rivers and loaded with anything from furniture to grain. The "mother ship" comes by periodically to pick up the barges and take them from one port to another. The "pick up" is literal: the LASH mother ship hoists the barges aboard, stowing as many as 45 below deck and 32 above.

DUNDALK-PATAPSCO NECK HISTORICAL SOCIETY

Beach scene at Sparrows Point, 1911.

Sparrows Point steel plant and shipyard, April 1940.

Company town . . . . The town of Sparrows Point, built in the early days of the steel plant, offered stores, banks, restaurants, six churches and cheap rent—$35 a month for six rooms—for plant workers. About 9,000 people lived here in the 1920s. Over the last several decades the town has been totally leveled to make room for the expanding plant.

DUNDALK-PATAPSCO NECK HISTORICAL SOCIETY

ROBERT F. KNIESCHE—MARYLAND HISTORICAL SOCIETY COLLECTION

Chapter 14

Sparrows Point

THOMAS Sparrow was granted a tract of land on the north side of the Patapsco River in 1652. He would hardly recognize the place today. One of the world's great steel mills, for many years Maryland's largest private employer, sprawls over 2,200 acres of land actually devoted to plant use. Importing ore from Seven Islands in Labrador, and bringing coal by barge from the Appalachians, the Bethlehem Steel Sparrows Point plant is capable of producing 7 million tons of steel annually. The plant's adjacent shipyard can produce tankers up to 300,000 deadweight tons.

Farmland until 1887, Sparrows Point was acquired by the Pennsylvania Steel Co. that year, and the first blast furnaces were producing pig iron by 1889. The shipyard was established in 1891. Bethlehem Steel acquired the plant and shipyard in 1916 and greatly expanded their respective capacities in subsequent years.

Plant owners have filled more than 1,400 acres of public waters since 1897 to create space for new furnaces, piers and storage, as can be seen by comparison of the two maps on the following page. The new land was free. Only since 1976 has the state

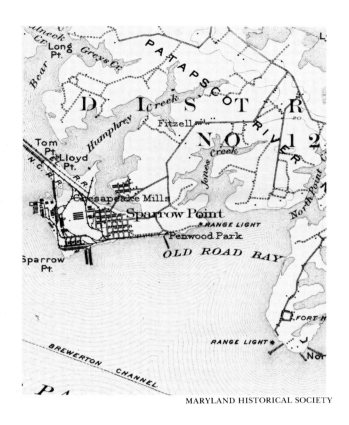

MARYLAND HISTORICAL SOCIETY

required compensation for taking public water, and the first Bethlehem application under the new rule, to fill in a 10-acre cove for coal storage, was made in 1981.

Two creeks border Sparrows Point, but neither offers much of interest to visitors.

Bear Creek, on the west side, is a curving creek with numerous branches, offering an opportunity for hundreds of persons, many of moderate income, to have a house and dock on the water. Repair yards and dockage are available at Lynch and Peachorchard coves; however, a series of draw bridges makes the creek inconvenient for sailboaters.

The sturdy Owens line of pleasure boats were built at Lynch Cove. The company was taken over by the Brunswick Co., and when wooden boat construction gave way to fiberglass, the plant was converted to the production of bowling alley floors. This business also has been discontinued.

Jones Creek and Old Road Bay border the Bethlehem plant on the East. The Young shipyard on Jones Creek has a tradition of construction and repair of wooden sailboats.

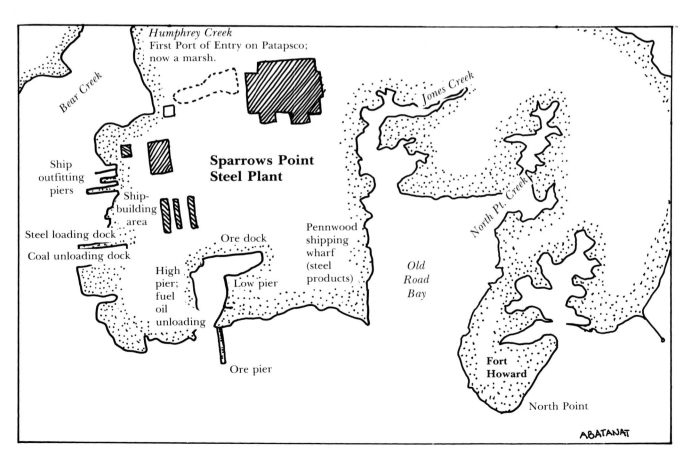

BALTIMORE GAS & ELECTRIC CO.

Sparrows Point shipyard (1958 view) .... Men have been building ships in this general vicinity on Bear Creek, near the mouth of the Patapsco River, for 300 years. More than 500 ships have come down the ways since the present Bethlehem yard was established in 1891. At right, workers prepare a new ship for launching.

ROBERT F. KNIESCHE

155

Launch-time approaches . . . . Sparrows Point workers knock over wooden supports used during construction. As the supports are removed, ship settles onto reusable launching cradles called poppets. (A stern poppet can be seen in the photo on the preceding page.) Tons of grease are applied to the slanted shipways. As the ship is christened, a handle is pulled at the side, triggering release of the cradles. Huge hydraulic rams emerge near the bow, in case the ship fails to slide down the ways of its own accord.

MARYLAND
HISTORICAL
SOCIETY
PHOTOS

Launching in a fog: Going . . . .

Dignitaries on the way to a Sparrows Point launching.

The big moment.

Going . . . .

Gone!

ROBERT F. KNIESCHE COLLECTION

DUNDALK-PATAPSCO NECK HISTORICAL SOCIETY PHOTOS

North Point, now home of Fort Howard Veterans Administration Medical Center . . . .
Roads at lower right lead to old gun emplacements shown in photograph below.

Chapter 15

North Point

NORTH Point and Old Road Bay offer the first sheltered anchorage for vessels entering the Patapsco River from the north. The earliest European colonists used the anchorage as a loading and distribution center for ocean-going vessels, before harbors were established further up the river. Small flat-bottomed boats brought tobacco hogsheads from points along the Patapsco and upper Chesapeake Bay and returned to their plantations with supplies from Europe.

Today North Point provides a tranquil setting for the Fort Howard Veterans Administration Medical Center, shown in the air view at left. The Fort, named for Col. John Eager Howard, a revolutionary hero and noted Baltimorean, was built in 1896 to defend Baltimore from possible naval attack. It remained under Army command until 1940. The old gun batteries are part of a shoreside park operated by the Baltimore County Department of Parks and Recreation. The park is closed during the winter, but the grounds of the fort are open year-round and afford a sweeping view of the river entrance and Chesapeake Bay.

Like Fort McHenry, North Point played a key role in the attempted siege of Baltimore during the War of 1812. On Sunday afternoon Sept. 11, 1814, three weeks after the sacking and burning of Washington, D.C., Admiral Cockburn's fleet arrived at the mouth of the Patapsco River, bent on subduing Baltimore and destroying her shipping, in retribution for the maraudings of the sleek Baltimore clippers.

Anchoring in Old Road Bay, the British fleet began landing troops and supplies on North Point early the next morning. At 7 a.m. a force of 4,700 soldiers, sailors and marines began the march on Baltimore. The master plan called for a simultaneous attack by water, employing the fleet to take out Fort McHenry and Lazaretto Point, while the land forces plundered the town and set fire to the shipyards.

Every American knows the star-spangled outcome: the leader of the British land force, Maj. Gen. Robert Ross, was dead of sniper bullets within hours of the landing; a 3,200-man Baltimore citizens militia, striking out from its campground at the junction of North Point road and the Philadelphia road, conducted an effective delaying action (the battle of North Point); the fortifications at Hampstead Hill (now Patterson Park) proved too strong for direct assault, and the British, looking for an opportunity to take them by flank, were compelled to stand around all night in a downpour. Because of shallow water and sunken obstacles, Cockburn's ships were unable to get close enough to conduct an effective bombardment of Fort McHenry. Perceiving this, the dispirited land forces stole back to North Point; and by dawn's early light of Sept. 14 it was clear to everyone that the attack had failed. The British troops were reboarding their ships as Francis Scott Key began penning his famous poem.

Cuckold Point

East of North Point is this ramshackle area of beer halls, boat ramps and outboard rentals, catering to the Millers Island fishing trade. On old maps it was called Cockles Point. A channel provides a shortcut to Middle River but deep-draft boats must avoid it.

The North Shore Parks

A SUCCESSION of resorts and amusement parks attracted Baltimoreans to the north shore of the Patapsco in earlier times. The *Samuel J. Pentz* brought patrons from Light Street to Holly Grove Park on Sparrows Point until the 1870s. Parks named Tivoli and Penwood were located on the same spot (see map, p. 154) in subsequent decades, until displaced by the expanding steel mill. At Tivoli Park on July 3, 1883 a rotted pier collapsed, plunging 300 persons into the water as they jammed up to board a tug-drawn barge for the return trip to the city. Sixty-three persons died, including 34 women and 23 children. Most of them were on an outing organized by the Corpus Christi Church in Mount Royal. It was the harbor's largest and most heartbreaking disaster in terms of loss of life.

In 1906, Bay Shore Park was opened to the east of North Point (see map, p. 11). It featured a 1,000-foot pier, a boardwalk, a roller coaster, a large pavilion, and a famous water merry-go-round that dunked its riders every few seconds. The park advertised "high class restaurants" and "no intoxicants." In 1947, Bethlehem Steel purchased the 900-acre track and tore down the buildings but made no effort to develop the land. The amusement equipment was moved to a new park, called Bay Island Beach, which was opened the following year on "Pleasure Island," just west of Hart Island. The resort was connected to Cuckold Point by causeway, and featured a casino, midway and bathhouse. It was purchased by Bethlehem Steel in 1964 and burned to the ground. The causeway was removed. Again the site was put to no use and can be visited by small boat.

The *Samuel J. Pentz* carried Baltimoreans to Holly Grove Park on Sparrows Point until the 1870s . . . . The *Pentz* is shown here on a later river freight run, location not known.

MARYLAND HISTORICAL SOCIETY

PEALE MUSEUM

This spindly roller coaster was one of the thrills at Bay Shore Park on North Point . . .
This view looks west, across Shallow Creek toward North Point Road.

The people-dipper . . . . Bay Shore Park's water merry-go-round is shown in this photo
taken about 1940. It dipped its riders in the water every few seconds.

DUNDALK-PATAPSCO NECK HISTORICAL SOCIETY

Chapter 16

Hart-Miller: The Dredging Project

(Map, page 11)

HART and Miller islands, flanking the northeast approach to the Patapsco River entrance, in 1987 began receiving the spoil from Baltimore's greatest harbor dredging project—a project tied up in controversy for over a decade. The purpose of the $400 million plan is to deepen the channel from Baltimore to Hampton Roads from 42 to 50 feet. This will enable large bulk carriers—ships carrying coal, grain, ore—to transport economical loads to or from Baltimore. For instance, Bethlehem Steel will be able to receive 125,000-ton iron ore carriers at Sparrows Point compared to the 65,000-tonners now in use, thus reducing by nearly half the number of ship visits necessary to feed its mills. Baltimore's competitive role in supplying European coal demands will be greatly enhanced. The relatively light displacement container and other breakbulk vessels will not be affected by the dredging. A depth of about 36 feet suffices for these ships at Dundalk Terminal today, less than the 42 feet already authorized. Nor is the dredging likely to result in a parade of large oil tankers up the Bay. With completion of the Colonial and Plan-

tation pipelines, much of Maryland's gasoline and light fuel oil now comes from the Gulf Coast to Baltimore by pipeline and its transport will not be affected by deepening of the ship channels.

Construction of a holding dike off Miller Island began late in 1981, using state funds. But the actual dredging was stalled until 1987 by controversy over how the estimated $240 million in costs would be apportioned among the state and federal government and users. With coal shipments down and the steel industry in disarray, the project seemed to lose much of its impetus by the time work began.

In previous years controversy raged over whether the project was safe environmentally. Residents along the shore facing the islands pointed to the foul nature of the materials to be dredged from the shipping lanes and dumped at the disposal site. Indeed, a researcher for the federal Environmental Protection Agency reported in 1978 that, as a result of industrial pollution, the muck at the bottom of Baltimore harbor contains more toxic heavy metals than anywhere else in the entire Chesapeake and Delaware Bay area. She found the level of toxic

RICHARD HOLDEN

Hart Island, with the west end of Miller Island visible at left, as seen from Rocky Point on the north shore. . . . The natural tranquility of this scene was altered forever when the islands were transformed into a disposal site. Eventually, officials say, the fill will be landscaped and made into a park.

sediments even worse than in Norfolk's filthy Elizabeth River: twice the amount of zinc, twice the cadmium, four times the lead, five times the copper and 11 times the chromium. "Hot spots" were found at the Inner Harbor, Colgate Creek, Bear Creek and Old Road Bay, near industrial installations. The researcher, Patricial G. Johnson, said the dangers posed by these metals if they enter the food chain are well documented. However, she said her research did not show whether the metals would cause damage if disturbed by dredging, or whether they would simply settle out again.

Court battles over use of the Hart-Miller site for disposal of the spoil ended in 1981, with the state winning permission to proceed with the plan. Hart-Miller was seen as the only practical site in the harbor large enough to receive the vast amounts of spoil which would be generated by scooping out eight feet of mud and sand at the bottom of the shipping channel.

Considering the pollution from industry, along with the debris and raw sewage brought down during heavy storms, one would almost expect Balti-more's harbor water to have the esthetic qualities of a cesspool. The reason this is not the case was discovered during a three-year study conducted by the Chesapeake Bay Institute of The Johns Hopkins University between 1958 and 1961. The study found that the harbor flushes itself far more rapidly than anyone would expect because of a layer of mixed water that moves out of the harbor at intermediate depths. It had been assumed that flushing was accomplished by the sluggish two-layer process which takes place elsewhere in the Bay, whereby salty bottom water slowly moves up the Bay, while fresher surface water slowly moves out. Instead, the researchers found that both bottom and top layers flow into Baltimore harbor, while the middle layer, of intermediate salinity and density, flows out. The surface layer of incoming low salinity or fresher water is driven primarily by the powerful Susquehanna River about 40 miles to the north. This unusual action, combined with in-and-out flows of the tides, causes 12 percent of the harbor water to be replaced with Bay water each day.

The Mud Machine

IN 1783, John and Andrew Ellicott built a wharf at Pratt and Light streets to export their flour. To deepen the water they used scoops drawn by horses and raised by windlass. This was the first dredging effort in Baltimore harbor. That same year, Maryland's colonial Assembly created a board of Port Wardens to manage the port and see to its dredging. Their greatest immediate challenge was to control Jones Falls and fill in the large marshy areas at its mouth. The wardens were authorized to levy a penny a ton on cargo entering and leaving the port (raised to 2 cents in 1788) in order to raise funds for dredging.

In 1790 the wardens approved the construction of the first "mud machine," a contraption operated by horses treading on a circular "horseway." The mud machine proved effective in digging mud from the harbor and placing it on a scow, but the unloading of the scow was slow and difficult. In 1827 the horses were replaced by a Watchman and Bratt steam engine—the first power-driven dredge—but this put expenses beyond the scope of the 2-cent user tax. Maryland's senior Senator, the Revolutionary hero Gen. Sam Smith, introduced a bill in Congress for the first time seeking federal assistance for Baltimore harbor dredging.

The Port Wardens were reduced to a single Warden in 1850; the individual was replaced by a Harbor Board in 1876, a structure which operated for 80 years until replaced by the Maryland Port Authority in 1956.

Dredging 200 years ago: the Mud Machine.

BALTIMORE MAGAZINE

Drawn for *Baltimore* by John McCormick

Dredging today: the disposal dike at Hart-Miller.

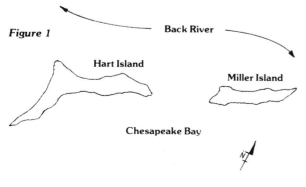

Figure 1

Back River

Hart Island

Miller Island

Chesapeake Bay

N

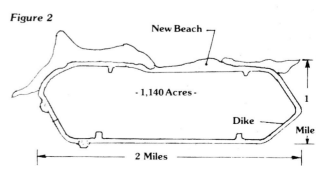

Figure 2

New Beach

- 1,140 Acres -

Dike

2 Miles

1 Mile

ROBERT F. KNIESCHE—MARYLAND HISTORICAL SOCIETY COLLECTION

Watching eclipse of the sun from Bay Island Beach, next to Hart Island, August 1951
. . . . The 105-foot tower at right is a range light for Craighill Channel. It guides ships
approaching Baltimore harbor from the south.

Two skipjacks and a bugeye head for the oyster beds in this dawn photo. Chesapeake
Bay is Maryland's richest treasure and one of the most prolific seafood producing bodies
in the world. Its protection from man's excesses is a continuing concern.

ROBERT F. KNIESCHE—MARYLAND HISTORICAL SOCIETY COLLECTION

Index

Ship Index

Other Readings

BALTIMORE AND CHESAPEAKE BAY

Steam Packets on the Chesapeake, a History of the Old Bay Line Since 1840, Alexander Crosby Brown, Cornell Maritime Press, Cambridge, Md., 1961.

Steamboats Out of Baltimore, Robert H. Burgess and H. Graham Wood, Tidewater Publishers, Cambridge, Md., 1968.

This Was Chesapeake Bay, Robert H. Burgess, Cornell Maritime Press, Cambridge, Md., 1963.

Chesapeake Circle, Robert H. Burgess, Cornell Maritime Press, Cambridge , Md., 1965.

Chesapeake Sailing Craft, Part 1, Robert H. Burgess, Tidewater Publishers, Cambridge, Md., l975.

PORT HISTORY

The Fells Point Story, Norman G. Rukert, Bodine & Associates, Inc., Baltimore, 1976.

Federal Hill, Norman G. Rukert, Bodine & Associates, Inc., Baltimore, 1980.

Historic Canton, Norman G. Rukert, Bodine & Associates, Inc., Baltimore, 1978.

The Port: Pride of Baltimore, Norman G. Rukert, Bodine & Associates, Inc., Baltimore, 1982.

Shipbuilding on the Patapsco, Parts l, 2, 3, 4 and 5, Ralph J. Robinson, *Baltimore* magazine, April, May, June, July, August l951.